WITHDRAWN

Poetry Brief

POETRY
BRIEF

An Anthology
of Short,
Short Poems

❦   *Edited by*
William Cole

The Macmillan Company
New York, New York

808.81

C

Copyright © 1971 by William Cole

All rights reserved. No part of this book may be reproduced or
transmitted in any form or by any means, electronic or mechanical,
including photocopying, recording or by any information storage and
retrieval system, without permission in writing from the Publisher.

The Macmillan Company
866 Third Avenue, New York, N.Y. 10022
Collier-Macmillan Canada Ltd., Toronto, Ontario

Library of Congress Catalog Card Number: 70–152286

First Printing

Printed in the United States of America

PROPERTY OF
TRINITY - PAWLING SCHOOL LIBRARY

*For arrangements made with various authors, their representatives, and
publishing houses who permitted the use of copyrighted material, the
following acknowledgments are gratefully made. All possible care has been
taken to trace the ownership of every selection included and to make full
acknowledgment for its use. If any errors have accidentally occurred, they
will be corrected in subsequent editions, provided notification is sent to
the editor in care of the publisher.*

Angus and Robertson for "Postage Stamp" from *The Talking Clothes*
by William Hart-Smith, and "Portrait" from *The Other Half* by
Judith Wright. Atheneum Publishers for "Spring Poem" from *The
Garbage Wars* by Donald Finkel. Copyright © 1969, 1970 by
Donald Finkel. "The Substituted Poem of Laureate Quynh" translated
W. S. Merwin with Nguyen Ngor Bich from *Selected Translations*,
1948–1968 by W. S. Merwin. Copyright © 1967 by W. S. Merwin.
"Separation" from *The Moving Target* by W. S. Merwin. Copyright ©
1963 by W. S. Merwin. "Accident on the Highway at Night" and

13.906

"One Sunday' from *The Storm and Other Poems* by William Pitt Root.
Copyright © 1967, 1968 by William Pitt Root. "Accident on the
Highway at Night" appeared originally in *Virginia Quarterly Review*.
"One Sunday" appeared originally in *West Coast Review*. COLEMAN BARKS
for "Body Poems": "Adams Apple," "Forehead," Testosterone," and
"Tic." BARRIE AND JENKINS LTD. for "At the End," "Coursegoules,"
"The Watch," and "Country Idyll" from *Collected Poems* by
Frances Cornford. GERARD BENSON for "Street Scene: St. John's Wood."
ANTHONY BLOND for "Saeva Senectus" from *The Worst Unsaid* by
T. S. Matthews. © T. S. Matthews. ROBERT BLY for "Love Poem" from
Silence in the Snowy Fields. Copyright © 1962 by Robert Bly. Reprinted
from *Silence in the Snowy Fields*, Wesleyan University Press, 1962. THE
BOBBS-MERRILL COMPANY, INC. for "Bronxus" from *In Time, Poems
1962–1968*. Copyright © 1969, by Joel Oppenheimer. TONY BUZAN
for "Disillusionment, Wordsworth." DAVID CALDER for "All the way to
the hospital" from *The Sunday Times* (London). JONATHAN CAPE LTD.
for "A Dying Man" from *A Trampolini* by Gael Turnbull. CHATTO
& WINDUS LTD. for "Shepherdess: A Love Poem" from *Collected Poems*
by Norman Cameron, and "The Full Heart" from *Ardours and
Endurances* by Robert Nichols. "Shepherdess: A Love Poem" is also
reprinted by permission of Alan Hodge. "The Full Heart" is also
reprinted by permission of Milton Waldman. CITY LIGHT BOOKS for
"The Last Supper" from *Paroles* by Jacques Prévert, translated by
Lawrence Ferlinghetti. Copyright © 1947 by Les Editions du Point
du Jour, Paris. THE COLLEGE ENGLISH ASSOCIATION for "Instructor's Folk
Carol" from *CEA Chap Book*, "Digressions and Indiscretions," by
Richard Leighton Greene.© 1968 by The College English Association.
COLLINS-KNOWLTON-WING, INC., for "A Last Poem" from *Man Is,
Women Does* by Robert Graves. Copyright © 1964 Robert Graves.
CHRISTOPHER CORNFELD for "Epitaph for Everyman" and "On the
Beach" from *On a Calm Shore* by Frances Cornfeld. CONTACT PRESS for
"I Sit Down to Write" from *A Local Pride* by Raymond Souster. Also
reprinted by permission of Raymond Souster. CURTIS BROWN LTD. for
"I am no Faust . . ." from *Exiles and Marriages* by Donald Hall.
Copyright © 1955 by Donald Hall. THE JOHN DAY COMPANY, INC. for
"Conversation in Gothic" from *Selected Verse* by John Manifold.
Copyright © 1946 by The John Day Company, Inc. DELACORTE PRESS
for "The Closing of the Rodeo" from *New and Selected Poems* by

William Jay Smith. Copyright © 1970 by William Jay Smith. A
Seymour Lawrence Book/Delacorte Press. ANDRE DEUTSCH LIMITED
PUBLISHERS for "Virtue" from *Collected Poems* by Ray Fuller.
DEVIN-ADAIR COMPANY for "To a Late Poplar" from *Collected Poems*
by Patrick Kavanaugh. Copyright 1964 by Patrick Kavanaugh: THE
DOLMEN PRESS for "Irish Curse on the Occupying English" from *A Heart
Full of Thought*, translated by Maire Mac Entee. DOUBLEDAY AND
COMPANY, INC. for "Birth Report" from *Growing Into Love* by
X. J. Kennedy. Copyright © 1965 by Burning Deck. "Said I Trusted
You" from *The Liverpool Scene* by Edward Lucie-Smith. Copyright
© 1967 by Edward Lucie-Smith. "Old Florist," "Heard in a Violent
Ward," and "Wish for a Young Wife" from *Collected Poems of
Theodore Roethke*. "Old Florist" copyright 1946 by Harper & Brothers;
"Heard in a Violent Ward," copyright © 1964 by Beatrice Roethke,
Administratrix of the Estate of Theodore Roethke; "Wish for a Young
Wife," copyright © 1963 by Beatrice Roethke, Administratrix of the
Estate of Theodore Roethke. "Uses of Poetry" from *New and Selected
Poems of Winfield Townley Scott*. Copyright © 1967 by Modern
Poetry Association. DUFOUR EDITIONS, INC. for "Delay" and "Fantasy"
from *Collected Poems 1967* by Elizabeth Jennings. © 1953, 1955,
1958, 1961, 1964, 1966, 1967 by Elizabeth Jennings. E. P. DUTTON &
Co., INC. for "Ezra" from *The Spirit of Place* by Lawrence Durrell.
Copyright 1969 © by Lawrence Durrell. "The Owl" from *The Zig Zag
Walk* by John Logan. Copyright © 1963, 1964, 1965, 1966, 1967,
1968, 1969 by John Logan. This poem originally appeared in *The Fair*.
EPOCH for "He, Then" by Paul Ramsay, and "I'm Married" by Eric
Torgersen. Copyright 1968 by Cornell University. "He, Then" is also
reprinted by permission of Paul Ramsay. "I'm Married" is also reprinted
by permission of Eric Torgersen. ETHEL ELLIS for "To James Who
Would Not Suffer Fools Gladly" and "Cuttlefish's Books" from
Mournful Numbers by Colin Ellis. EYRIE AND SPOTTISWOODE
(PUBLISHERS) LTD. for "After Love" from *Poems 1942–67* by Alan Ross.
GAVIN EWART for "Epitaph (Of his wife's character . . .)." FABER
AND FABER LIMITED for "The Invitation" from *The Hungry Grass* by
Donagh Mac Donagh. ANGEL FLORES for "Fate" by Christian
Morgenstern, translated by R. F. C. Hull, from *An Anthology of German
Poetry*, edited by Angel Flores, "I Am François, to my Dismay," from
An Anthology of Medieval Lyrics, edited by Angel Flores. GRANADA

Publishing Limited for "A Day in Autumn" from *Poetry for Supper*
and "Farm Child" from *Song at the Year's End* by R. S. Thomas,
and "The Nest" and "A Dead Mole" from *The Collected Poems* by
Andrew Young. Hamish Hamilton Ltd. for "Epitaph for a Columnist"
from *The Fern on the Rock* by Paul Dehn. Copyright © 1965 by
Paul Dehn: Hamish Hamilton, London. Harcourt Brace Jovanovich,
Inc. for "The Smiles of the Bathers" from *The Fall of the Magicians*
by Weldon Kees. Copyright, 1947. "Epitaph #10 & Epitaph #12"
from *Poems of C. S. Lewis* edited by Walter Hooper, copyright © 1964
by the Executors of the Estate of C. S. Lewis. "My Sons" from
Meat Air by Ron Loewinsohn. Copyright © 1970 by Ron Loewinsohn.
"Envoi" from *The Contemplative Quarry* by Anna Wickham. "The
Proof" from *Waking to Sleep* by Richard Wilbur. Copyright 1964 by
Richard Wilbur. Harper & Row Publishers, Inc. for "They Call Me"
from *Poems* by Yehuda Amichai. Translated from the Hebrew by
Assia Gutmann. Copyright © 1968 by Yehuda Amichai; English
translation copyright © 1968, 1969 by Assia Gutmann. "Passing
Remark" from *The Rescued Year* by William Stafford. Copyright
© 1961 by William E. Stafford. Geof Hewitt for "State of the Union
(1970)." David Higham Associates, Ltd. for "For Johnny" from
Collected Poems by John Pudney; also for "After Shakespeare" and
"Emily" from *Haste to the Wedding* by Alex Comfort. Hill and Wang,
Inc. for "Elegy V" from *Dolphins at Cochin* by Tom Buchan. Copyright
© 1969 by Tom Buchan. "The Projectionist's Nightmare" from *Notes
to the Hurrying Man* by Brian Patten. © Brian Patten, 1969. John
Hollander for "Stooping for Salad" by John Hollander. Holt, Rinehart
and Winston, Inc. for "They say my verse is said: no wonder" and
"Yonder see the morning blink:" from *The Collected Poems of A. E.
Housman.* Copyright 1922 by Holt, Rinehart and Winston, Inc.
Copyright © 1964 by Robert E. Symons. "Still Lifes—I" by Reuben
Iceland, translated by Etta Blum and "Poem" by Celia Dropkin,
translated by Adrienne Rich from *A Treasury of Yiddish Poetry* edited
by Irving Howe and Eliezer Greenberg. "Bravado," "Nothing Gold
Can Stay," "A Patch of Old Snow," and "Lodged" from *The Poetry of
Robert Frost* edited by Connery Lathem. Copyright 1916, 1923, 1928,
1947, © 1968 by Holt, Rinehart and Winston, Inc. Copyright 1944
1951, © 1956 by Robert Frost. The Horizon Press for "Early Astir"
from *Selected Writings* by Herbert Read, and "Garden Party" and

"Epitaph" from *Collected Poems* by Herbert Read; and "Ode" from *Collected Poems* by Basil Bunting. EDWARD NEWMAN HORN for "Man and wife the night resume . . ." and "Inscribed in the Heidelberg Visitor's Book" from *Poems in Places*. ALFRED A. KNOPF, INC. for "The Poet as Troublemaker" reprinted from *The Wreck of the Thresher* by William Meredith. Copyright © 1964 by William Meredith. HOUGHTON MIFFLIN COMPANY for "Philoctetes" from *Laughing* by Paul Hannigan. Copyright © 1970 by Paul Hannigan. "Timeo" from *Birthdays from the Ocean* by Isabella Gardner McCormick. Copyright 1951, 1952, 1953, 1954, 1955 by Isabella Gardner McCormick. "Housewife" from *All My Pretty Ones* by Anne Sexton. Copyright © 1961, 1962 by Anne Sexton. R. G. HOWARTH for "Gushing Guest" and "Pest" from *Very Good for Me*. Copyright © 1969 by R. G. Howarth. GERALD JONAS for "Bird-Fear." First published in *Poetry Northwest*. KAYAK for "The Boss Hires" from *What the Grass Says* by Charles Simic. MARY KENNEDY for "Con Dolore" from *Ride Into Morning* published by The Gotham Book Mart. Copyright © 1969 by Mary Kennedy. LADYSMITH PRESS for "Albatross" by Marnie Pomeroy. THE LISTENER for "Good-Night" by Seamus Heaney and "De Trop" by Alan Dixon. LITTLE, BROWN AND COMPANY for "Avanti, Gourmetti!" from *There's Always Another Windmill* by Ogden Nash. Copyright © 1968 by Ogden Nash. "Small Space" and "Athens, Ohio, 1939" from *Scattered Returns* by L. E. Sissman. Copyright © 1966, 1967, 1968, 1969, by L. E. Sissman. LONDON MAGAZINE PUBLICATIONS for "It's Already Autumn" from *Contemporary Italian Poetry* by Elio Pagliarani © London Magazine. "Fairy Tale Reversed" by B. Gutteridge from *London Magazine*, March 1970, © London Magazine. "Morning in Madrid" from *Collected Poems*, Bernard Spencer. © Alan Ross Ltd. LOUISIANA STATE UNIVERSITY PRESS for "The King's Men" from *Depth of Field* by William Heyen. Copyright © 1969 by William Heyen. LEWIS MACADAMS, JR., for "After the Wafer" from *The Young American Poets*. Copyright 1970 Lewis MacAdams, Jr. WILLIAM MACLELLAN PUBLISHERS LTD. for "Mars and Venus at Hogmanay" from *The Deevil's Waltz* by Sydney Goodsir Smith. MACLELLAND AND STEWART LIMITED for "Curaçao" from *Selected Poems* by Earle Birney. MACMILLAN for "Grotto, and Recollection" from *Ingestion of Ice-Cream* by Geoffrey Grigson, and for "For Jane Bradley, with a Porringer" by Hal Summers from *Ten Poets of Our Time*, edited by James M. Charlton. THE

MACMILLAN COMPANY for "A Thunderstorm in Town" from *Collected Poems* by Thomas Hardy. Copyright 1925 by The Macmillan Company. "Waiting Both" from *Collected Poems*, by Thomas Hardy. Copyright 1925 by The Macmillan Company, renewed 1953 by Lloyds Bank, Ltd. "Being Born and a Few Consequences" (Part III) from *Rubrics for a Revolution* by John L'Heureux. Copyright © 1964 by John L'Heureux. "The Bonnie Broukit Bairn" and "The Two Parents" from *Collected Poems* by Hugh MacDiarmid. © 1948, 1962 Christopher Murry Grieve. "Now Philippa Is Gone" from *Selected Poems* by Anne Ridler. Copyright © 1950, 1951, 1952, 1953, 1961 by Anne Ridler "An Inscription by the Sea" from *Collected Poems* by Edwin Arlington Robinson. Copyright 1915 by Edwin Arlington Robinson, renewed 1943 by Ruth Nivison. "Maples in Autumn" from *The Shrinking Orchestra* by William Woods. © 1961, 1963 by William Woods. "The Old Men Admiring Themselves in the Water" from *Collected Poems* by William Butler Yeats. Copyright 1903 by The Macmillan Company, renewed 1931 by William Butler Yeats. "All Things Can Tempt Me" from *Collected Poems* by William Butler Yeats. Copyright 1912 by The Macmillan Company, renewed 1940 by Bertha Georgie Yeats. "Father and Child" from *Collected Poems* by William Butler Yeats. Copyright 1933 byThe Macmillan Company, renewed 1961 by Bertha Georgie Yeats. "The Great Day," "A Stick of Incense," and "The Chambermaid's First Song" from *Collected Poems* by William Butler Yeats. Copyright 1940 by Georgie Yeats, renewed 1968 by Bertha Georgia Yeats, Michael Butler Yeats and Anne Yeats. THE MARVELL PRESS for "Wants," "Wires," and "Absences" from *The Less Deceived* by Philip Larkin. © copyright The Marvell Press 1955, 1970. WILLIAM MATCHETT for "The Edge of the Island" from *Water Ouzel* by William H. Matchett. Copyright 1955 by William Matchett. METHUEN AND CO. LTD. for "Trout Leaping in the Arun Where a Juggler Was Drowned" from *Poor Man's Riches* by Charles Dalmon. BERT MEYERS for "For W. R. Rodgers" by Bert Meyers. WILLIAM MORROW AND COMPANY, INC. for "The Cry" from *The Burning Field* by Mark Perlberg. Copyright © 1960, 1961, 1962, 1963, 1965, 1966, 1967, 1969 by Mark Perlberg. LISEL MUELLER and *Poetry* for "A Poem About the Hounds and the Hares," which was first published in *Poetry*. LEONARD NATHAN for "Judgment" from *Shenandoah*. © 1970 by *Shenandoah: The Washington and Lee University Review*. The poem is also reprinted by permission of *Shenandoah*. THE NATION for "Small as a Fist" by Ryah Tumarkin Goodman, and for "Midsummer" by H. R. Hays. THE NEW STATESMAN (London) for "Small, Smaller" by Russell Hoban. NEW DIRECTIONS PUBLISHING CORPORATION for "Roller Coaster" and "The Imperfect Lover" from *Poems and Antipoems* by Nicanor Parra. Copyright © 1966, 1967 by Nicanor Parra. "Pagani's, November 8," "The Faun," and "And the days are not full enough . . ." from *Personae* by Ezra Pound. Copyright 1926 by Ezra Pound. "I Remember" from *Selected Poems* by Stevie Smith. Copyright © 1964 by Stevie Smith. "North Beach Alba" from *The Back Country* by Gary Snyder. Copyright © 1957 by Gary Snyder. THE NEW YORKER for "November" by John Falstaff. Copyright © 1933, 1961. "In Passing" by Gerald Jonas. © 1966 The New Yorker Magazine, Inc. "The Pollard Beech" by Laurie Lee from *Laurie Lee*. Copyright © 1950 The New Yorker Magazine, Inc. Also reprinted by permission of Laurie Lee. "Upon Shaving Off One's Beard" by John Updike. © 1970 The New Yorker Magazine, Inc. "Midsummer Night's Dream" by Mildred Weston. Copyright © 1932, 1960 The New Yorker Magazine, Inc. ALAN NOWLAN for "God Sour the Milk of the Knacking Wench." OCTOBER HOUSE, INC. for "Zimmer's Head Thudding Against the Blackboard" by Paul Zimmer from *The Republic of Many Voices*. Copyright © 1969 by Paul Zimmer. OXFORD UNIVERSITY PRESS (Canadian Branch) for "The Plowman in Darkness" from *The Boatman* by Jay Macpherson. OXFORD UNIVERSITY PRESS (London) for "Prelude" by J. M. Synge from *The Collected Works of J. M. Synge*, and for "Lesson" from *The Stones of Emptiness* by Anthony Thwaite. OXFORD UNIVERSITY PRESS, INC. (New York) for "For a Lamb" from *Collected Poems 1930–1960* by Richard Eberhart. © 1960 by Richard Eberhart. "Scaffolding" from *The Death of a Naturalist* by Seamus Heaney. © 1966 by Seamus Heaney. "As in Their Time" (Part X) and "Aubade" from *The Collected Poems of Louis MacNeice*, edited by E. R. Dodds. Copyright © The Estate of Louis MacNeice 1966. "War Song of the Embattled Finns" from *Root and Branch* by Jon Stallworthy. © Jon Stallworthy, 1969. A. D. PETERS & COMPANY for "The Early Morning," "The Face," and "On Hygiene" from *Sonnets and Verse* by Hilaire Belloc. "A Memory" from *Selected Poems* by L. A. G. Strong. RANDOM HOUSE, INC. for "Those boys ran together," "Robert," and "Love rejected" from *Good Times* by Lucille Clifton. Copyright © 1969 by Lucille Clifton. "Days" from *The Whitsun Weddings* by Philip Larkin. Copyright © 1964 by Philip Larkin. "Suddenly" from *Ruining the New Road* by William Matthews. Copyright © 1970 by William Matthews. RAPP AND WHITING for "Without Laying Claim" from *The Awakening* by William Wantling. HENRY REGNERY COMPANY for "Fishing Boats in Martigues" from *Collected Poems* by Roy Campbell. MURIEL RUKEYSER for "In Our Time." ST. MARTIN'S PRESS, INC. for "Old Words" from *The Skylark* by Ralph Hodgson. G. T. SASSOON for "Base Details" by Siegfried Sassoon. SATURDAY REVIEW for "The First War" by William Stafford. Copyright 1964 Saturday Review, Inc. ELEANOR M. SCOTT for "Let us Record" from *Biography for Traman*. CHARLES SCRIBNER'S SONS for "Love Comes Quietly" from *For Love* by Robert Creeley. Copyright © 1962 Robert Creeley. MARTIN SECKER & WARBURG LIMITED, PUBLISHER for "The Party" and "The Lovers" from *Awake and Other Poems* by W. R. Rodgers. SHEL SILVERSTEIN for "Early Bird" by Shel Silverstein. © 1971 Shel Silverstein. MICHAEL SILVERTON for "What Is Poetry?" LOUIS SIMPSON for "The Wall Test." THE SOCIETY OF AUTHORS, London, for "The Spotted Flycatcher" and "Night" from *Collected Poems* by Walter de la Mare. STONY BROOK POETICS FOUNDATION for "The Original Elk Hotel & Bar" by Geoffrey O'Brien and "Sijo" by Robert Vas Dias. Copyright © 1969 by Stony Brook Poetics Foundation. THE SWALLOW PRESS, INC. for "My dear, though I have left no sign . . . ," "With every wife he can . . . ," "Soft found a way" from *The Exclusions of a Rhyme* by J. V. Cunningham. © 1960. "Cradle Song" and "Girl Help" from *Poems 1924–1944* by Janet Lewis. © 1950. "Writing While My Father Dies" from *New Poetry Anthology II* by Linda Pastan. © 1971. TURRET BOOKS for "The Ladybirds" from *Six Kinds of Creatures* by Edward Lucie-Smith. © Edward Lucie-Smith, 1969. TWAYNE PUBLISHERS for "Cats" from *Selected Poems of Gunnar Ekelof*. Copyright 1967. UNIVERSITY OF PITTSBURGH PRESS for "Short Moral" and "To My Daughter" from *First Practice* by Gary Gildner. © 1969 by the University of Pittsburgh Press. "Christmas Eve Wish" from *Body Compass* by David Steinglass. © 1969 by the University of Pittsburgh Press. THE VIKING PRESS for "Things Men Have Made . . . ," "Spray," "Leda," and "Good Husbands Make Unhappy Wives" from *The Complete Poems of D. H. Lawrence*, Volume I, edited by Vivian de Sola Pinto and F. Warren Roberts. Copyright 1929 by Frieda Lawrence. "Gift" and "Go by Brooks" by Leonard Cohen from *Selected Poems: 1956–1968* by Leonard Cohen. Copyright in all countries of the International Copyright Union. "Aware" by D. H. Lawrence, Volume I of *The Complete Poems of D. H. Lawrence*, edited by Vivian de Sola Pinto and F. Warren Roberts. Copyright 1920 by B. W. Huebsch, Inc., renewed 1948 by Frieda Lawrence. "Tourists" by D. H. Lawrence from *The Complete Poems of D. H. Lawrence*, Volume II, edited by Vivian de Sola Pinto and F. Warren Roberts. Copyright 1933 by Frieda Lawrence. "A Jellyfish" from *The Complete Poems of Marianne Moore*. WESLEYAN UNIVERSITY PRESS for "The Way We Live" from *The Stone Harp* by John Haines. Copyright © 1968 by John Haines. "New-Born" from *To Make Me Grieve* by Molly Holden. Reprinted from *To Make Me Grieve*, Phoenix Living Poets Series. "The Curates" from *A Sense of Being* by John Horder. Copyright © 1968 by John Horder. "Display Window" from *Cairns* by Christopher Levenson. Copyright © 1969 by Christopher Levenson. "See That One?" from *Madonna of the Cello* by Robert Bagg. Copyright © 1968 by Robert Bagg. "Prayer to the Snowy Owl" from *Winter News* by John Haines. Copyright © 1963 by John Haines. "The Gardener" from *Winter News* by John Haines. Copyright © 1965 by John Haines. "Gardeners" from *Rescue the Dead* by David Ignatow. Copyright 1966 by David Ignatow. "North" from *Night Light* by Donald Justice. Copyright © 1967 by Donald Justice. "On the Death of Friends in Childhood" from *The Summer Anniversaries* by Donald Justice. Copyright © 1959 by Donald Justice. "I fear to take a step . . ." from *Kinds of Affection* by Josephine Miles. Copyright © 1965 by Josephine Miles. "An Answer of Sorts" from *The Day the Perfect Speaker Left* by Leonard Nathan. Copyright © 1967 by Leonard Nathan. "Sunday Morning" from *Battle Report* by Harvey Shapiro. Copyright © 1963 by Harvey Shapiro. WESTERN WASHINGTON STATE COLLEGE for "To a Young Poet" by X. J. Kennedy from *Concerning Poetry No. 1*. THE JARGON SOCIETY for "Aunt Creasy, On Work" from *The New York Times*. Copyright 1971 by Jonathan Williams. Reprinted from *Blues & Roots/Rue & Bluets*. PETE WINSLOW for "Form" and "Peter, Peter . . ." from *Whatever Happened to Pete Winslow?* Copyright © 1960 by Pete Winslow and for "Cheap Valentine" which appeared in *Extension No. 1*. Copyright © 1968 by Suzanne Zavrian and Joachim Neugroschel. THE WORLD PUBLISHING COMPANY for "Hesitate to Call" from *Firstborn* by Louise Gluck. Copyright © 1968 by Louise Gluck.

Contents

Introduction

In 1968 I published a collection of short, short poems under
the descriptive title *Eight Lines and Under*. These were
poem on the same theme, and the compact idea, the
the years. This present collection differs; these poems
didn't accrete; they were actively sought out by going
through a poetry library of some two thousand volumes,
from Abse to Zaturenska, and by checking another
three hundred anthologies.

The internationality of this collection wasn't intentional;
it just happened. Most of the poems are American and
English, but there is representation as well from Australia,
Canada, Scotland, and Ireland, and translations from the
Spanish, German, French, Italian, and Yiddish. Not many
translations, though; a translation is really a different
poem on the same theme; and the compact idea, the
flashing image, of a short poem is hard to translate.

In this collection, my restrictions on length are looser. In
the earlier book, I cheated occasionally and went to
ten—and even eleven—lines. Here, I've generally tried
to hold to ten lines, but when tempted easily gave in and
went to extreme lengths—twelve and thirteen lines.

This book is also longer; there are almost three hundred poems; a painful winnowing down from six hundred that had been found and typed. An anthologist has a right to his prejudices; there are no limericks here, and only one poem of a Japanesy nature has slipped in. There are no "nothing poems," as I call them. These are unsubtle bits, usually on domestic frustrations or passing topical phenomena, once dear to the readers (or editors) of *The Saturday Evening Post* and the ladies' magazines. A contemporary nothing poem might be: "One thing that really hurts my eyes/Is mini-skirts on maxi-thighs." Well, okay, but that "hurts my eyes" is forced in to "rhyme it all up." In a good short poem, especially a rhyming one, every word must work, must pull an oar in the boat.

Another kind of poem that is missing through pure prejudice is the automatic-writing kind of thing now so popular. At the risk of being regarded as a middle-aged fogy, I admit that I see no virtue in the school loosely known as the "New York" school of poets. Instant poetry—add a teaspoonful of your friends' names and stir. Only occasionally does a proper poem come out of them, and then seemingly by accident.

About a third of the contemporary poems here were found in magazines. I am a compulsive reader of all kinds of magazines, particularly poetry magazines. Incidentally, one thing America doesn't need right now is another poetry magazine. There are too many outlets for mediocre poets; some improvement in the existing magazines would help. England, alas, very much needs a poetry magazine; the poets there have pitifully few outlets: the fine *London Magazine*; the rather disgraced *Encounter*; the few literary-political weeklies. *Punch* could, but doesn't, fill the same role in printing poetry that the *New Yorker* fills here.

The first anthology of any kind ever compiled was an anthology of short poems; known as "The Greek Anthology," it was a collection of epigrams, graffiti, songs, and epitaphs written by known and unknown Greeks from the fifth century B.C. to the sixth century A.D. Why was this collection all short poems? They were originally cut on stones, and, as any stonecutter will tell you, keep it short. Making translations of the poems in "The Greek Anthology" is still a favorite avocation of Greek scholars.

While *Poetry Brief* is, inadvertently, a brief for the short poem, it is not primarily that. It is for enjoyment; these poems are jabs in the ribs, jolts of likening, spurts of excitement. They have something of interest to say, and brevity is the soul of it. But enough—to the kernels! I borrow an exit line from Ben Jonson:

> Wouldst thou hear what man can say
> In a little? Reader, stay.

William Cole

I

❧

*"When we
are in
love"*

❧ Love Poem

When we are in love, we love the grass,
And the barns, and the lightpoles,
And the small mainstreets abandoned all night.
>   *Robert Bly*

❧ Postage Stamp

If you should ever have to
part from someone dear, tear
yourself away, be sure

the tear is where
the perforations are. Please,
please do not ever

recklessly sever, sheer
yourself from some one other
so that their stamp is torn

and you have part of their
living, bleeding
flesh at your side worn.
>   *William Hart-Smith*

🌷 Father and Child

She hears me strike the board and say
That she is under ban
Of all good men and women,
Being mentioned with a man
That has the worst of all bad names;
And thereupon replies
That his hair is beautiful,
Cold as the March wind his eyes.

William Butler Yeats

🌷 He, Then

No, she said. Please, she said.
He tasted her hunger, his fingers
touching her ear lobe, the flesh behind it.
None the less, he did not kiss her.
In the hallway and down the stairs he trembled
with the hurt of his leaving.
In the raw snow blowing in the wind,
in the slide of the water loosing,
he said, Please, he said Please, in the snow.

Paul Ramsey

🌱 The Lovers

After the tiff there was silence, till
One word, flung in centre like single stone,
Starred and cracked the ice of her resentment
To its edge. From that stung core opened and
Poured up one outward and widening wave
Of eager and extravagant anger.

>   W. R. Rodgers

🌱 The Imperfect Lover

A pair of newlyweds
Halt before a tomb
She is in severe white.

To observe without being seen
I hide behind a pillar.

While the sad bride
Weeds her father's grave
The imperfect lover devotes himself
To reading a magazine.

>   *Nicanor Parra*
>   *Translated from the Spanish by Miller Williams*

Albatross

Around my neck I keep the dead love tied
Like a festering Albatross
To learn to loath it: if bound close
It can't beat into life and rend my side.

Marnie Pomeroy

A Thunderstorm in Town
(A Reminiscence: 1893)

She wore a new "terra-cotta" dress,
And we stayed, because of the pelting storm,
Within the hansom's dry recess,
Though the horse had stopped; yea, motionless
We sat on, snug and warm.

Then the downpour ceases, to my sharp sad pain
And the glass that had screened our forms before
Flew up, and out she sprang to her door:
I should have kissed her if the rain
Had lasted a minute more.

Thomas Hardy

🌷 Said I Trusted You

said I trusted you
spoke too soon
heard of your affair
with the maninthemoon
say it's all over
then if you're right
why does he call
at the house every night?

        Roger McGough

🌷 Gift

    You tell me that silence
is nearer to peace than poems
but if for my gift
I brought you silence
(for I know silence)
you would say
    This is not silence
this is another poem
and you would hand it back to me.

        Leonard Cohen

🌿 Leda

Come not with kisses
not with caresses
of hands and lips and murmurings;
come with a hiss of wings
and sea-touch tip of a beak
and treading of wet, webbed, wave-working feet
into the marsh-soft belly.

D. H. Lawrence

🌿 After Shakespeare

At the end of the third act, poetry gutters down—
at eleven, the best pentameters drag their feet;
Tragedy sinks to some old pother
and we find ourselves holding hands in the street,
suddenly tired of eloquence overdone
and wondering why we went, who have each other
in flesh and no pretense. We'll let the great dead stay dead.

That first act of our own
is still the best act left. Let's go to bed.

Alex Comfort

🌹 The Original Elk Hotel & Bar

My wife's dog
makes a leap

right for my testicles . . .
That dog,
she loves my wife.

She loves my wife!

   Geoffrey O'Brien

🌹 The Chambermaid's First Song

How come this ranger
Now sunk in rest,
Stranger with stranger,
On my cold breast?
What's left to sigh for?
Strange night has come;
God's love has hidden him
Out of all harm,
Pleasure has made him
Weak as a worm.

   William Butler Yeats

🌵 Hesitate to Call

Lived to see you throwing
Me aside. That fought
Like netted fish inside me. Saw you throbbing
In my syrups. Saw you sleep. And lived to see
That all that flushed down
The refuse. Done?
It lives in me.
You live in me. Malignant.
Love, you ever want me, don't.

       Louise Glück

🌵 Delay

The radiance of that star that leans on me
Was shining years ago. The light that now
Glitters up there my eye may never see,
And so the time lag teases me with how

Love that loves now may not reach me until
Its first desire is spent. The star's impulse
Must wait for eyes to claim it beautiful
And love arrived may find us somewhere else.

       Elizabeth Jennings

❦ Old Words

—Say that over!
"The loved one and the lover."
—Words now one never hears;
Once more over—
"The loved one and the lover."
—Strange they sound to modern ears!

    Ralph Hodgson

❦ Shepherdess
   (A *love poem*)

All day my sheep have mingled with yours. They strayed
Into your valley seeking a change of ground.
Held and bemused by what they and I had found,
Pastures and wonders, heedlessly I delayed.

Now it is late. The tracks leading home are steep,
The stars and landmarks in your country are strange.
How can I take my sheep back over the range?
Shepherdess, show me now where I may sleep.

    Norman Cameron

🌷 Separation

Your absence has gone through me
Like thread through a needle.
Everything I do is stitched with its color.

> W. S. Merwin

🌷 Scaffolding

Masons, when they start upon a building,
Are careful to test out the scaffolding;

Make sure that planks won't slip at busy points,
Secure all ladders, tighten bolted joints.

And yet all this comes down when the job's done
Showing off walls of sure and solid stone.

So if, my dear, there sometimes seem to be
Old bridges breaking between you and me

Never fear. We may let the scaffolds fall
Confident that we have built our wall.

> Seamus Heaney

❦ Aunt Creasy, On Work:

shucks
I make the livin'
uncle
just makes the livin'
worthwhile

>   *Jonathan Williams*

❦ Poem

You sowed in me, not a child
but yourself.
So it's you growing in me daily,
greater and more distinct.
There's no room left inside me
for myself
and my soul lies like a dog at your feet
growing fainter and fainter.
But, dying into you,
I still, even now, can make you songs.

>   *Celia Dropkin*
>   *Translated from the Yiddish by Adrienne Rich*

❦ *Midsummer Night's Dream*

Embodied souls
In pairs,
In honeyed twos
Frequent the parks,
Essay the avenues,
Wondering what deity
Could be invoked
That they'd be joined together
Yet not yoked.

Mildred Weston

❦ *Love Comes Quietly*

Love comes quietly,
finally, drops
about me, on me,
in the old ways.

What did I know
thinking myself
able to go
alone all the way.

Robert Creeley

With every wife he can, and you know why?
Bold goes to bed because really he's shy.
And why I publish it none knows but I:
I publish it because really I'm shy.

  J. V. Cunningham

Go by Brooks

Go by brooks, love,
Where fish stare,
Go by brooks,
I will pass there.

Go by rivers,
Where eels throng,
Rivers, love,
I won't be long.

Go by oceans,
Where whales sail,
Oceans, love,
I will not fail.

  Leonard Cohen

❦ A Stick of Incense

Whence did all that fury come?
From empty tomb or Virgin womb?
Saint Joseph thought the world would melt
But liked the way his finger smelt.

William Butler Yeats

❦ After Love

After love, to continue the caress
Is both to insure
Against sadness and to reassure
The one and the other that "Yes"
Has not become "No,"
And the urge to get up and dress,
Leave a kiss on the brow, and go,
Is one that will subside
In the slowly returning tide
That brings us to the next caress
True elements of tenderness.

Alan Ross

❦ *Suddenly*

The truth is out, and nothing
is the same. You are
the last surprise, I am
an elk come too far south,
puzzled by villages.
Too late, too late, I run
through snowy fields
on melting legs.

       William Matthews

❦ *Cheap Valentine*

I guess I like you
Even though you have no legs and must wear 80 pairs of stockings

I knew your breasts were peculiar
Now one of them has exploded, ruining a sweater
I was disgusted to see you had given birth to a cigarette

Your eyes are demanding
I'm sorry, I don't have 23 thousand owls
But I guess I like you.

       Pete Winslow

❦ It's Already Autumn

It's already autumn, and I've suffered other months
without learning anything
except that I lost you
for too much love like a hungry man
overturning the bowl
with his trembling hands.

> Elio Pagliarani
> *Translated from the Italian by G. Singh*

❦ Fairy Tale Reversed

Yes, said the Shepherdess lying with the Prince
You may have my hymen for the price of a quince
And if you put it in slowly I'll promise not to wince.

In slipped the Prince's tool, a soft hard hot rod,
O sighed the Shepherdess I've got me a Mod God
My eyes in the heavens and my bum on a pillow sod.

Then as his weapon magicked Gog and Magog
It turned from its living blood to an icy elm log
And his hands on her breasts were the flippers of a Frog.

> *Bernard Gutteridge*

II

*"How soft
were their pelts,
how graceful
their leaps"*

A Poem about the Hounds and the Hares

After the kill, there is the feast.
And towards the end, when the dancing subsides
and the young have sneaked off somewhere,
the hounds, drunk on the blood of the hares,
begin to talk of how soft
were their pelts, how graceful their leaps,
how lovely their scared, gentle eyes.

Lisel Mueller

Con Dolore

Small birds are frozen in the river:
Huddled in inadequate feathers they are scattered upon the ice.
Unable to fly further against descending cold
They came down to rest upon the water.
Dark forces trapped both birds and river in the night.
The frozen river is as helpless as they are.
You, who have wings, why should you perish?
Who seizes the pattern knows the reason.

Mary Kennedy

🌷 A Dead Mole

Strong-shouldered mole,
That so much lived below the ground,
Dug, fought and loved, hunted and fed,
For you to raise a mound
Was as for us to make a hole;
What wonder now that being dead
Your body lies here stout and square
Buried within the blue vault of the air?

Andrew Young

🌷 Wires

The widest prairies have electric fences,
For though old cattle know they must not stray,
Young steers are always scenting purer water
Not here but anywhere. Beyond the wires

Leads them to blunder up against the wires
Whose muscle-shredding violence gives no quarter.
Young steers become old cattle from that day,
Electric limits to their widest senses.

Philip Larkin

🌷 Sijo

Where is that place where the home
   is, he is, the hermit crab
cold wanderer and perennial
   borrower, never building
and always moving in or
   moving out, finding the fit.

     Robert Vas Dias

🌷 The Owl
    (After János Hegedüs and for Jill Bullitt)

The moon is in sight
On a poplar rotting in the night
Two lamps of eyes catch fire
Two clawed feet clutch at their desire
The profound owl
Ferocious and gray
Grotesquely feeds
For he is hungry as can be
He is hungry as can be.

     John Logan

🌷 Early Bird

Oh if you're a bird, be an early bird
And catch the worm for your breakfast plate
If you're a bird, be an early bird
But if you're a worm, sleep late.

Shel Silverstein

🌷 On Buying a Dog

"I wish to buy a dog," she said,
"A dog you're sure is quite well bred,
In fact, I'd like some guarantee
He's favored with a pedigree."

"My charming friend," the pet man said,
"I have a dog that's so well bred,
If he could talk, I'll guarantee
He'd never speak to you or me."

Edgar Klauber

🌷 The Faun

Ha! sir, I have seen you sniffing and snoozling about among my
   flowers.
And what, pray, do you know about horticulture, you capriped?
"Come, Auster, come, Apeliota,
And see the faun in our garden.
But if you move or speak
This thing will run at you
And scare itself to spasms."

    Ezra Pound

🌷 Cats

A cat is not a person, you say,
not a Christian—
I have seen many!
Playing with mice who sat on their tails squeaking out protest
Then let them go
to die by themselves of shock
without wounds other than small claw-marks
little love-bites

    Gunnar Ekelöf
    Translated from the Swedish by Muriel Rukeyser and Lief Sjöberg

🌻 The Cry

The buoy clangs offshore, indolently.
Fog, born above the sea, slips over the island's outer ledges.
A vessel, dipping into swells, disappears,
Then rides up and is visible again, from where I watch,
As it slides past the point toward its mooring.
On the beach a crow, raking through a holiday of garbage,
Raises its head and cries terribly in the air.

Mark Perlberg

🌻 The Ladybirds

The fretful ladybirds complain
On being often sent on vain
And foolish errands—safe and sound
Their children sleep; their houses wait
(Instead of burning to the ground)
With docile fires in the grate.

They are ungrateful. What a relief
Never to find expected grief!

Edward Lucie-Smith

🌷 Fate

The Lightning spoke one stormy night:
"O wretched sheep, I bring you light!"

The poor sheep, cowering blindly back
Had rump and left side burned jet black.

Since then it's spent its days in gloom;
Why did that happen, and from whom?

> *Christian Morgenstern*
> *Translated from the German by R. F. C. Hull*

🌷 For a Lamb

I saw on the slant hill a putrid lamb,
Propped with daisies. The sleep looked deep,
The face nudged in the green pillow
But the guts were out for crows to eat.

Where's the lamb? whose tender plaint
Said all for the mute breezes.
Say he's in the wind somewhere,
Say, there's a lamb in the daisies.

> *Richard Eberhart*

🌷 A Jellyfish

Visible, invisible,
   a fluctuating charm
an amber-tinctured amethyst
   inhabits it, your arm
approaches and it opens
   and it closes; you had meant
to catch it and it quivers;
   you abandon your intent.

     Marianne Moore

🌷 Country Idyll

Deep in the stable tied with rope,
The cow has neither dignity nor hope.

With ugly, puzzled, hot despair
She needs the calf that is not there,
And mourns and mourns him to unheeding air.

But if the sleeping farmer hears,
He pulls the blanket higher round his ears.

     Frances Cornford

❧ The Nest

Four blue stones in this thrush's nest
I leave, content to make the best
Of turquoise, lapis lazuli
Or for that matter of the whole blue sky.

Andrew Young

❧ Garden Party

I have assumed a conscious sociability,
pressed unresponding hands,
sipped tea,
and chattered aimlessly
all afternoon,

Achieving spontaneity
only
when my eyes lit at the sight
of a scarlet spider
running over the bright
green mould of an apple tree.

Herbert Read

❦ Bird-Fear

Bird-fear, fear of the fall, of the season's fall, the feather's fall,
the year's toll, the wind's call; fear of the pale sun, the bare field,
the bare branch; fear of death by frost, by hard ground in a dry
   time.
By storm's siege; fear of the sea, the city, night-fog, quick-lime;
fear of the cat, the silent stalker, the nest-spoiler, the neck-breaker;
fear of the snake, the leaf-lurker; fear of the hawk, of the sharp beak
and sharp claw; fear of the long reach of man, the steely-cold
   sight—
Bird-fear, bird-fear, fear of the cage, fear of the air, the price of
   flight.

Gerald Jonas

🌸 The Spotted Flycatcher

Gray on gray post, this silent little bird
Swoops on its prey—prey neither seen nor heard!
A click of bill; a flicker; and, back again!
Sighs Nature an *Alas*? Or merely, *Amen*?

>   Walter de la Mare

🌸 Midnight

Midnight's bell goes ting, ting, ting, ting,·
Then dogs do howl, and not a bird does sing
But the nightingale, and she cries twit, twit, twit:
Owls then on every bough do sit;
Ravens croak on chimney's tops;
The cricket in the chamber hops,
　　And the cats cry mew, mew, mew.
The nibbling mouse is not asleep,
But he goes peep, peep, peep, peep,
　　And the cats cry mew, mew, mew,
　　And still the cats cry mew, mew, mew.

>   Thomas Middleton

❦ Ode

A thrush in the syringa sings.

"Hunger ruffles my wings, fear,
lust, familiar things.

Death thrusts hard. My sons
by hawk's beak, by stones,
trusting weak wings
by cat and weasel, die.

Thunder smothers the sky.
From a shaken bush I
list familiar things,
fear, hunger, lust."

O gay thrush!
Basil Bunting

🌷 Small, Smaller

I thought that I knew all that there was to know
Of being small, until I saw once, black against the snow,
A shrew, trapped in my footprint, jump and fall
And jump again and fall, the hole too deep, the walls too tall.

    Russell Hoban

🌷 Lesson

In the big stockyards, where pigs, cows, and sheep
Stumble towards the steady punch that beats
All sense out of a body with one blow,
Certain old beasts are trained to lead the rest
And where they go the young ones meekly go.

Week after week these veterans show the way,
Then, turned back just in time, are led themselves
Back to the pens where their initiates wait.
The young must cram all knowledge in one day,
But the old who lead live on and educate.

    Anthony Thwaite

🌷 On the Beach

On what pure mission do the seagulls fly,
A flock of delegates across the sky?
There goes, I think, their Minister of State,
Supremely calm, though just a little late.

Frances Cornford

🌷 Prayer to the Snowy Owl

Descend, silent spirit;

you whose golden eyes
pierce the grey
shroud of the world—

Marvelous ghost!

Drifter of the arctic night,
destroyer of those
who gnaw in the dark—

preserver of whiteness.

John Haines

III

❦

*"That's my muse
at her
typewriter"*

🌷 *Spring Poem*
   (After Han Shan)

My parents left me a pretty fair living
I needn't envy any man his measure

clack clack   that's my muse at her typewriter
yakety-yak   my kids in the garden

the petals come clattering down
my heart capers in his cave

or I sit with my chin on my fist
and listen to the jays

and who comes to my party?
well   sometimes the cat.

   Donald Finkel

🌷 *The Poet as Troublemaker*

She likes to split an apple down the middle
And with her hands behind her ask them, which?
The other children fall in with the riddle
But he says, both hands! both hands you sly old bitch!

   William Meredith

❧ *All Things Can Tempt Me*

All things can tempt me from this craft of verse:
One time it was a woman's face, or worse—
The seeming needs of my fool-driven land;
Now nothing but comes readier to the hand
Than this accustomed toil. When I was young,
I had not given a penny for a song
Did not the poet sing it with such airs
That one believed he had a sword upstairs;
Yet would be now, could I but have my wish,
Colder and dumber and deafer than a fish.

William Butler Yeats

Good friend, for Jesus' sake forbear
To dig the dust enclosed here.
Blest be the man that spares these stones,
But curst be he that moves my bones.

Epitaph on Shakespeare's tomb

 To Sir George Ethridge
On his Shewing his Verses Imperfect

Be wise, and ne'er to publick View produce
Thy undrest Mistress, or unfinisht Muse;
Since either, by that *Dishabilé*, seem
To hurt their Beauties in our good Esteem:
And easier far we kind Impressions make,
Than can we rooted Prejudices shake,
From Nature learn, which *Embrio's* does conceal,
Thine, till they're perfect, never to reveal.

William Wycherley

Form

Peter Peter Pumpkin Eater
Is trochaic tetrameter.

> *Pete Winslow*

Roller Coaster

For half a century
Poetry was the paradise
Of the solemn fool.
Until I came
And built my roller coaster.

Go up, if you feel like it.
I'm not responsible if you come down
With your mouth and nose bleeding.

> *Nicanor Parra*
> *Translated from the Spanish by Miller Williams*

❦ I Sit Down to Write

I sit down to write
a poem about you, but my good right hand
keeps getting up from the desk and running across
the hall to the bedroom where you are sleeping

and stealing under the covers
takes your breasts for a moment's rioting.

    Raymond Souster

❦ After an Interval
    (November 22, 1875, Midnight—Saturn and Mars in Conjunction)

After an interval, reading, here in the midnight,
With the great stars looking on—all the stars of Orion looking,
And the silent Pleiades—and the duo looking of Saturn and ruddy
    Mars;
Pondering, reading my own songs, after a long interval, (sorrow
    and death familiar now)
Ere Closing the book, what pride! what joy! to find them
Standing so well the test of death and night,
And the duo of Saturn and Mars!

    Walt Whitman

✿ What Is Poetry?

A person of my acquaintance asked me one evening,
"What is poetry, Michael?"
"Poetry," I explained,
"is like a pump for your bicycle tires.
Poetry," I explained, "is wonderful.
Look," I said,
"imagine that you have been thrown from the roof by gangsters.
Where would you find solace?
In poetry!
You would do well to read poetry all the time."
To signal the close of my lecture
I drew and parried a little silver sword
I carry at my side for such purposes.

Michael Silverton

I Am François, to My Dismay

I am François, to my dismay,
Parisian born, out Pontoise way,
And through the lesson ropes convey
My neck'll learn what my arse may weigh.

François Villon
Translated from the French by Harvey Birenbaum

They say my verse is sad: no wonder;
  Its narrow measure spans
Tears of eternity, and sorrow,
  Not mine, but man's.

This is for all ill-treated fellows
  Unborn and unbegot,
For them to read when they're in trouble
  And I am not.

A. E. Housman

🌷 On a Day's Stint

And long ere dinner-time I have
  Full eight close pages wrote.
What, Duty, hast thou now to crave?
  Well done, Sir Walter Scott!

    Sir Walter Scott

🌷 A Memory

When I was as high as that
I saw a poet in his hat.
I think the poet must have smiled
At such a solemn gazing child.

Now wasn't it a funny thing
To get a sight of J. M. Synge,
And notice nothing but his hat?
Yet life is often queer like that.

    L. A. G. Strong

🌷 In Our Time

In our period, they say there is free speech.
They say there is no penalty for poets,
There is no penalty for writing poems.
They say this.   This is the penalty.

Muriel Rukeyser

🌷 The Invitation

The horse of poetry nibbles
The summer-riddled grass,
Lifting his heavy head
To the young girls as they pass;

Riderless he may drowse
Till the year turn over.
Leap girl upon his back
And he will race for ever.

Donagh MacDonagh

Love poems they read
Were work of an aging man
Alone and celibate
Who published them in joy
Of his craftsman's skill,
How they folded into each other.

Many a lust-starched boy
Read them aloud to his girl
Till her widening eyes darkened
Till her breath trembled thin
Till the boy threw down the book
And they folded into each other.

Winfield Townley Scott

Heard in a Violent Ward

In heaven, too,
You'd be institutionalized.
But that's all right,—
If they let you eat and swear
With the likes of Blake,
And Christopher Smart,
And that sweet man, John Clare.

Theodore Roethke

Emily

There was a storm over Maine. It came that way:
it felled a tree. It left great desolation.
Emily Dickinson swept the lightning up
and stuck the terrible things in her pincushion.

In time she fed birds again, and made jam in Fall,
but she hid herself from tradesmen when they came—
and what she had in her workbasket
she never showed to anyone at all.

Alex Comfort

🌷 A Last Poem

A last poem, and a very last, and yet another—
O, when can I give over?
Must I drive the pen until the blood bursts from my nails
And my breath fails and I shake with fever?
Shall I never hear her whisper softly,
"But this is one written by you only,
And for me only; therefore, love, have done"?

    Robert Graves

🌷 Art Thou Heywood

Art thou Heywood with the mad mery wit?
Ye forsooth maister, that same is even hit.
Art thou Heywood that applieth mirth more then thrift?
Ye sir, I take mery mirth a golden gift.
Art thou Heywood that hath made many mad plaies?
Ye many plaies, fewe good woorkes in all my daies.
Art thou Heywood that hath made men mery long?
Ye: and will, if I be made mery among.
Art thou Heywood that woulde be made mery now?
Ye sir: helpe me to it now I beseche yow.

    John Heywood

🌷 After the Wafer

House of Cards, House of Dreams,
Oboes, bassoons, sisters, brothers,
I think my head is falling off now.   off

> *Lewis MacAdams*

🌷 Zimmer's Head Thudding Against the Blackboard

At the blackboard I had missed
Five number problems in a row,
And was about to foul a sixth,
When the old, exasperated nun
Began to pound my head against
My six mistakes. When I cried,
She threw me back into my seat,
Where I hid my head and swore
That very day I'd be a poet,
And curse her yellow teeth with this.

> *Paul Zimmer*

🌷 *The Quidditie*

My God, a verse is not a crown,
No point of honor, or gay suit,
No hawk, or banquet, or renown,
Nor a good sword, nor yet a lute:

It cannot vault, or dance, or play;
It never was in France or Spain;
Nor can it entertain the day
With my great stable or demain:

It is no office, art, or news,
Nor the Exchange, or busie Hall;
But it is that which while I use
I am with thee, and most take all.

> *George Herbert*

IV

*"The world's
a jest"*

Senex to Matt. Prior

Ah! Matt.: old age has brought to me
Thy wisdom, less thy certainty:
The world's a jest, and joy's a trinket:
I knew that once: but now—I think it.

J. K. Stephen

State of the Union (1970)

On my portable color tv
Richard, red fisted
Grows yellow and smiles.
I return him to off-white.
He needs new countries to bomb.

Brinkley is green, apologetic,
His partners darken at the local news,
And purple men become
Believable as words.

Geof Hewitt

🌷 Avanti, Gourmetti!

Sea horses may be Romanized
By calling them hippocampi;
If you would do the same to shrimp,
Add garlic, and they're scampi.

Ogden Nash

🌷 Mars and Venus at Hogmanay

The nicht is deep,
The snaw liggs crisp wi rime,
Black an cauld the leafless trees;
Midnicht, but nae bells chime.

Throu the tuim white sleepan street
Mars an Venus shauchle past,
A drucken jock wi a drucken hure
Rairan "The Ball o Kirriemuir"!

Sydney Goodsir Smith

liggs: lies
tuim: empty, deserted
shauchle: shuffle, stumble
rairan: roaring

I have no pain, dear Mother, now,
But, oh, I am so dry;
So connect me to a brewery,
And leave me there to die.

Anonymous

 The Last Supper

They are at table
They eat not
Nor touch their plates
And their plates stand straight up
Behind their heads.

Jacques Prévert
Translated from the French by Lawrence Ferlinghetti

🌱 *Small Space*

I
MEN PAST 40
GET UP NIGHTS
And look out at
City lights,
Wondering where they
Made the wrong
Turn, and why life
Is so long.

II
WOMAN NEARLY
ITCHED TO DEATH
As her body,
Filled with breath,
Tortured her with
Womanly
Longing, wholly
Humanly.

III
MAKE THESE THREE
MISTAKES IN SPEECH?
Hear them mermaids
On the beach
Singing real low
Each to each?
Had I ought to
Eat a peach?

L. E. Sissman

🌷 The Choir Boy

And when he sang in choruses
  His voice o'ertopped the rest,
Which is very inartistic,
  But the public like that best.

Anonymous

🌷 L'Enfant Glacé

When baby's cries grew hard to bear
I popped him in the Frigidaire.
I never would have done so if
I'd known that he'd be frozen stiff.
My wife said: "George, I'm so unhappé!
Our darling's now completely *frappé*!"

Harry Graham

🌷 Impromptu Poem

The Bishop of Chester,
Though wiser than Nestor
And fairer than Esther,
If you scratch him will fester.

Thomas Gray

🌷 Disgusting

At the boarding house where I live
Things are getting very old.
Long gray hairs in the butter,
And the cheese is green with mold,
When the dog died we had sausage
When the cat died catnip tea.
When the landlord died I left it;
Spareribs are too much for me.

Anonymous

🌷 French and English

The French have taste in all they do,
  Which we are quite without;
For Nature, that to them gave *goût*,
  To us gave only gout.

> *Thomas Erskine*

🌷 The Irish Colonel

Said the King to the Colonel:
"The complaints are eternal,
  That you Irish give more trouble
Than any other corps."

Said the Colonel to the King:
"This complaint is no new thing,
  For your foemen, Sire, have made it
A hundred times before."

> *A. Conan Doyle*

Found Poem
From *The Hound of the Baskervilles*

I stooped, panting, and pressed my pistol
  To the dreadful, shimmering head,
But it was useless to press the trigger,
  The giant hound was dead.

    A. Conan Doyle

Charms and a man I sing, to wit—a most superior person,
Myself who bears the fitting name of George Nathaniel Curzon.
From which 'tis clear that even when in swaddling bands I lay low,
There floated round my head a sort of apostolic halo.

    Lord Curzon

❦ Found Poem
From *Elementary Treatise on Mathematics* (1819)

And no force, however great,
Can stretch a cord, however fine,
Into a horizontal line
That shall be absolutely straight.

> *William Whewell*

❦ Disillusionment, Wordsworth

I lay as did Will,
half asleep and quite still,
in the song of the birds a-delighting.

I opened my eyes,
and to my surprise,
I found that the bastards were fighting.

> *Tony Buzan*

🌸 Instructor's Folk Carol

Promotion Day is coming in a little while:
Please to drop a volume on the chairman's pile;
If you haven't got a volume, an article will do;
If you haven't got an article, God help you!

Richard Leighton Greene

🌸 Stanzas

When a man hath no freedom to fight for at home,
　　Let him combat for that of his neighbors;
Let him think of the glories of Greece and of Rome,
　　And get knocked on the head for his labors.

To do good to Mankind is the chivalrous plan,
　　And is always as nobly requited;
Then battle for Freedom wherever you can,
　　And, if not shot or hanged, you'll get knighted.

George Gordon, Lord Byron

🌷 Passing through the Carron Iron Warks

We cam na here to view your warks,
   In hopes to be mair wise,
But only, lest we gang to Hell,
   It may be nae surprise.

   Robert Burns

🌷 The Projectionist's Nightmare

This is the projectionist's nightmare:
A bird finds its way into the cinema,
finds the beam, flies down it,
smashes into a screen depicting a garden,
a sunset and two people being nice to each other.
Real blood, real intestines, slither down
the likeness of a tree.
"This is no good," screams the audience,
"This is not what we came to see."

   Brian Patten

🌷 On Hygiene

Of old when folk lay sick and sorely tried
The doctors gave them physic, and they died.
But here's a happier age: for now we know
Both how to make men sick and keep them so.

Hilaire Belloc

🌷 Inscribed in the Heidelberg Visitor's Book

I came to Germany to see
My old professor's family.
The family is dead and gone,
The old professor carries on
With a bride of twenty-two
And two children that are new.
Live and learn from my professor:
To learn ist gut, to live ist besser.

Edward Newman Horn

❦ *Body Poems*

Adam's Apple

never said
a word:

he just nodded

Forehead

the two main lines
of your palm fit
exactly over the ones
at the top of the
bridge of your nose:

what have you forgotten

Testosterone

the secret additive
ingredient:

godamighty Harriet
let's slow down

Tic

talk to me
talk to me

Coleman Barks

V

❧

*"I like
girls human and
sunlight hot"*

🌷 *Conversation in Gothic*
(Bonn-am-Rhein, 1939)

The thin trees shiver, the Rhine runs cold;
This soil will never bear gum or gold.

The pale sun slackens, the dark descends,
And Undine beckons with slim, pale hands.

"No use, young woman, though thanks a lot;
I like girls human and sunlight hot,

"Brown skin, red clarets that rasp the mouth;
You have your merits, but I go south."

The dark stream surges; with angry tears
Undine submerges and disappears.

  John Manifold

🌷 *No Difference i'th'Dark*

Night makes no difference 'twixt the Priest and Clark;
Jone as my Lady is as good i'th'dark.

Robert Herrick

🌷 *See That One?*

See that one with tanned arms, nice hips,
Joking with the soda jerk?
See how her nipples perk
Out her blouse when she sips
Her soda, and her shoulder slips

Into view when he teases her?
You want to pick her up?
Would you mind her make-up,
How her sentences slur,
Or, curled up in a car, her purr?

Robert Bagg

Imitation of Pope: A Compliment to the Ladies

Wondrous the Gods, more wondrous are the Men,
More Wondrous Wondrous still the Cock & Hen,
More Wondrous still the Table, Stool & Chair;
But Ah! More wondrous still the Charming Fair.

William Blake

Judgment

When my women (you can count them off on one hand)
Foregather in Heaven to judge and make me a Hell,
Unstitching my life and holding the pieces up
For a laugh among friends, I will stare down at my feet
Like a country boy and be grateful, for what if they turned
Their backs or forgot how once I troubled them? Dozens
Of poems, a million unpublished words, and countless
Caressing silences—all for a little attention.
O, I'd stand there unstitched, loving the way they undid me
Down to the bone where their names are committed as praise.

Leonard Nathan

❦ *Sous-Entendu*

Don't think

that I don't know
that as you talk to me
the hand of your mind
is inconspicuously
taking off my stocking,
moving in resourceful blindness
up my thigh.

Don't think
that I don't know
that you know
everything I say
is a garment.

Anne Stevenson

From you, Ianthe, little troubles pass
   Like little ripples down a sunny river;
Your pleasures spring like daisies in the grass,
   Cut down, and up again as blithe as ever.

   Walter Savage Landor

🌷 *My Sons*

I'll teach my sons
         the same as me—LOOK
at those girls on the bus to work
         intimations of real
warm bloodgiving flesh,
         comfortable, moving
beneath the cloth . . .
. . . to fill our days with beauty
from whatever faucet's available.

   Ron Loewinsohn

🌷 *I'm Married*
—a letter to the folks

My wife has tattoos on her neck
and queer, unmatching breasts.
She's very young, and plays
barbaric music on the radio.

She's in the john now,
washing my socks in the bathtub
and singing to herself.

When I'm late at night
she comes and sits down on my lap
and scribbles on what I'm writing,

I'm very happy.

Eric Torgersen

❦ Lines Written in an Ovid

Ovid is the surest guide,
   You can name, to show the way
To any woman, maid, or bride,
   Who resolves to go astray.

    Matthew Prior

❦ Upon the Nipples of Julia's Breast

Have ye beheld (with much delight)
A red rose peeping through a white?
Or else a cherry (double grac'd)
Within a lily? Centre plac'd?
Or ever mark'd the pretty beam,
A strawberry shows half drown'd in cream?
Or seen rich rubies blushing through
A pure smooth pearl, and orient too?
So like to this, nay all the rest,
Is each neat niplet of her breast.

    Robert Herrick

Old World Dialogue

"Is this," she asked, "what the lower orders call . . .?"
"Yes, yes," replied her lover, Lord Whitehall,
"But hush! the expression is a trifle crude—"
"*Much* too good for them," cried Lady Ermintrude.
"Nevertheless" resumed the tactless peer,
"Those who excel at it—pray do not sneer—
Are, by and large, of obscure parentage.
    One girl I knew—"
        "Take that!" she shouted, blind with rage.

Robert Graves

The Substituted Poem of Laureate Quynh

This is what the professor wrote home, listen:
tell my wife not to get heated up.
I have got all the way north here perfectly limp.
Down south there she had better look to her clam.
Is it still tight and winding like a gopher's burrow
or is it gaping by now like a catfish grotto?
Tell her to hang onto it even if it gives her a fight.
I will be home in a couple of days.

Anonymous Vietnamese folk poem
Translated by W. S. Merwin with Nguyen Ngoc Bich

🌷 Epitaph

Of his wife's character he sadly said:
Whore in the kitchen—and a cook in bed.

Gavin Ewart

🌷 Curaçao

I think I am going to love it here

I ask the man in the telegraph office
the way to the bank
He locks the door and walks with me
insisting he needs the exercise

When I ask the lady at my hotel desk
what bus to take to the beach
she gives me a lift with her beautiful sister
who is just driving by in a sports job

And already I have thought of something
I want to ask the sister

Earle Birney

all the way to the hospital
for my twentieth transfusion
i thought of you, darling,
and your funny lovebites.

David Calder

 Wish for a Young Wife

My lizard, my lively writher,
May your limbs never wither,
May the eyes in your face
Survive the green ice
Of envy's mean gaze;
May you live out your life
Without hate, without grief,
And your hair ever blaze,
In the sun, in the sun,
When I am undone,
When I am no one.

Theodore Roethke

🌷 Pagani's, November 8

Suddenly discovering in the eyes of the very beautiful
Normande cocotte
The eyes of the very learned British Museum assistant.

    Ezra Pound

🌷 Display Window

In full view of the fashionable shoppers
A sleek young man on padded feet assaults
The tailor's dummies behind plate glass. Perfunctorily
Flowered hat, veil and fifty-guinea coat
Slip from the model's elegant shoulders, revealing
Unnippled naked breasts, smooth thighs of plaster.
Finally even the wig goes. Yet these practised girls
Shrug off their humiliation, hands still beckon and wave
Invisible umbrellas or toy with prancing poodles. Though
Bald now and blatantly sexless, they retain their poise.
The furry customers shudder and pass on.

    Christopher Levenson

VI

*"Life folds
like a fan
with a click!"*

Epitaph

Yes yes
and ever it will come to this:
Life folds like a fan with a click!
The hand that lately beat the air
with an arch of painted silk
falls listless in the lap.

The air
the agitation and the flush
close and collapse. A rigid frame
restricts the limbs that once ran free
across the heath across the fields
over the threatening hills.

> *Herbert Read*

###

My mammy kill me,
My daddy eat me,
All my brudders and sisters pick my bones,
And throw them under the marble stones.

> *Negro folk rhyme*

Vain the ambition of kings
Who seek by trophies and dead things,
To leave a living name behind,
And weave but nets to catch the wind.

John Webster

🌷 A *Dying Man*

Some compulsion to ask:
"Is there anything you want?"

afraid of his answer
for there's nothing I can give,

ashamed of my question
knowing he knows,

forgiven by a lie,
his merciful, "No."

Gael Turnbull

My dear, though I have left no sigh
Carved on your stone, yet I still cherish
Your name and your flesh will not die
Till I and my descendants perish.

> J. V. Cunningham

 An Inscription by the Sea
(After a poem in the "Greek Anthology")

No dust have I to cover me,
  My grave no man may show;
My tomb is this unending sea,
  And I lie far below.
My fate, O stranger, was to drown;
And where it was the ship went down
  Is what the sea birds know.

> *Edwin Arlington Robinson*

🌷 On Grizzel Grim

Here lies with death auld Grizzel Grim,
   Lincluden's ugly witch;
O death, how horrid is thy taste,
   To lie with such a bitch!

    Robert Burns

🌷 For Johnny

Do not despair
For Johnny-head-in-air;
He sleeps as sound
As Johnny underground.

Fetch out no shroud
For Johnny-in-the-cloud;
And keep your tears
For him in after years.

Better by far
For Johnny-the-bright-star,
To keep your head,
And see his children fed.

    John Pudney

❦ Trout Leaping in the Arun Where a Juggler Was Drowned

His flesh and bones have long since gone,
But still the stream runs gaily on.
And still his merry ghost contrives
To juggle with his silver knives.

  Charles Dalmon

❦ Writing While My Father Dies

There is not a poem in sight,
only my father running out
upstairs, and me without a nickel
for the meter. The children hide
before the television
shivering in its glacial light,
and shivering I rub these words
together, hoping for a spark.

  Linda Pastan

🌷 Epitaph

Erected by her sorrowing brothers
In memory of Martha Clay.
Here lies one who lived for others;
Now she has peace. And so have they.

    C. S. Lewis

🌷 For W. R. Rodgers
    (1909–1969)

I knew a candle of a man
whose voice, meandering in a flame,
could make the shadows on the wall
listen to what he said.
Time flowed from a vein that ran
like a blue crack through his pale forehead.

He's done. You'd need a broom
to arouse him now.
All things burn before they're dead.
Some men were words that warmed a room.

    Bert Meyers

the End

my great-aunt Sarah died, how I remember well,
alone with daffodils and never rang her bell.
as quiet as her chair and books upon her shelf.
e no trouble to her nurse, no trouble to herself.
s more quiet than the bare, ploughed fields that lay outside.
nowledge in her listening face as certain was, and wide.

Frances Cornford

The King's Men

hat is it, inside them and undeniable,
at mourns him? that drives them, searching
or the moon-shaped tracks of his horse,
a glint of armor within a maze of pines?

He'd know their barbarous need would never wane.
They will keep on to the next horizon,
where he waits. They will keep on, lowering
their barred visors against the setting sun.

William Heyen

On the Death of Friends in Childhood

We shall not ever meet them bearded in heaven,
Nor sunning themselves among the bald of hell;
If anywhere, in the deserted schoolyard at twilight,
Forming a ring, perhaps, or joining hands
In games whose very names we have forgotten.
Come, memory, let us seek them there in the shadows.

Donald Justice

The Knight's Tomb

Where is the grave of Sir Arthur O'Kellyn?
Where may the grave of that good man be?—
By the side of a spring, on the breast of Helvellyn,
Under the twigs of a young birch tree!
The oak that in summer was sweet to hear,
And whistled and roared in the winter alone,
Is gone,—and the birch in its stead is grown.—
The Knight's bones are dust,
And his good sword rust;—
His soul is with the saints, I trust.

Samuel Taylor Coleridge

In Passing

Open-backed dumpy junktruck
stacked full of old floor-fans,
unplugged, unsteady, undone,
free-whirling like kids' pinwheels
in a last fresh breeze—
What a way to go!

Gerald Jonas

War Song of the Embattled Finns
1939

Snow inexhaustibly
falling on snow! Those whom
we fight are so many,
Finland so small,
where shall we ever find room
to bury them all?

Jon Stallworthy

Ezra

Ci-git Ezra
Who knew ten lang
    But could not choo
When writing Englis
    Which to use.

Lawrence Durrell

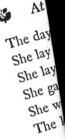

At

The day
She lay
She lay
She ga
She w
The

They Call Me

Taxis below
And angels above
Are impatient.
At one and the same time
They call me
With a terrible voice.

I'm coming, I am
Coming,
I'm coming down,
I'm coming up!

Yehuda Amichai
Translated from the Hebrew by Assia Gutn

❦ Epitaph for Everyman

My heart was more disgraceful, more alone,
And more courageous than the world has known.

O passer-by, my heart was like your own.
> *Frances Cornford*

❦ A Memorial Poem
Illness is to reconcile us to death

Week after week, month after month, in pain
You wrestled with that fiendish enemy—
The thing that tried in vain
To drag you from the room to its own territory.

Each day renewed the duel and our grief
Until at last upon the crumpled bed—
To our unwished relief—
The strange emaciated brown-faced fiend lay dead.
> *Roy Fuller*

Now Philippa Is Gone

Now Philippa is gone, that so divinely
Could strum and sing, and is rufus and gay,
Have we the heart to sing, or at midday
Dive under Trotton Bridge? We shall only
Doze in the yellow spikenard by the wood
And take our tea and melons in the shade.

Anne Ridler

Elegy

When I am burned and by arrangement
scattered on the earth
I shall remain a year or two inside your head
until it too is burned
and then we shall remain (not quite ourselves!)
only inside the heads of those who knew us
till they in turn are dead
and then we shall be nothing.

Tom Buchan

VII

"Wind, Water, Stars, and Night"

❦ On the Death of Friends in Childhood

We shall not ever meet them bearded in heaven,
Nor sunning themselves among the bald of hell;
If anywhere, in the deserted schoolyard at twilight,
Forming a ring, perhaps, or joining hands
In games whose very names we have forgotten.
Come, memory, let us seek them there in the shadows.

Donald Justice

❦ The Knight's Tomb

Where is the grave of Sir Arthur O'Kellyn?
Where may the grave of that good man be?—
By the side of a spring, on the breast of Helvellyn,
Under the twigs of a young birch tree!
The oak that in summer was sweet to hear,
And whistled and roared in the winter alone,
Is gone,—and the birch in its stead is grown.—
The Knight's bones are dust,
And his good sword rust;—
His soul is with the saints, I trust.

Samuel Taylor Coleridge

🌷 In Passing

Open-backed dumpy junktruck
stacked full of old floor-fans,
unplugged, unsteady, undone,
free-whirling like kids' pinwheels
in a last fresh breeze—
What a way to go!

Gerald Jonas

🌷 War Song of the Embattled Finns
1939

Snow inexhaustibly
falling on snow! Those whom
we fight are so many,
Finland so small,
where shall we ever find room
to bury them all?

Jon Stallworthy

❧ Ezra

Ci-git Ezra
Who knew ten languages
  But could not choose
When writing English poetry
  Which to use.

    Lawrence Durrell

❧ They Call Me

Taxis below
And angels above
Are impatient.
At one and the same time
They call me
With a terrible voice.

I'm coming, I am
Coming,
I'm coming down,
I'm coming up!

      Yehuda Amichai
      Translated from the Hebrew by Assia Gutmann

🌺 At the End

The day my great-aunt Sarah died, how I remember well,
She lay alone with daffodils and never rang her bell.
She lay as quiet as her chair and books upon her shelf.
She gave no trouble to her nurse, no trouble to herself.
She was more quiet than the bare, ploughed fields that lay outside.
The knowledge in her listening face as certain was, and wide.

Frances Cornford

🌺 The King's Men

What is it, inside them and undeniable,
that mourns him? that drives them, searching
for the moon-shaped tracks of his horse,
a glint of armor within a maze of pines?

He'd know their barbarous need would never wane.
They will keep on to the next horizon,
where he waits. They will keep on, lowering
their barred visors against the setting sun.

William Heyen

92

ᰧ   from *Reconciliation*

Word over all, beautiful as the sky,
Beautiful that war and all its deeds of carnage must in time be
    utterly lost,
That the hands of the sisters Death and Night incessantly softly
    wash again, and ever again, this soiled world.
    Walt Whitman

ᰧ   from *Song of Myself*

I believe a leaf of grass is no less than the journeywork of the stars,
And the pismire is equally perfect, and a grain of sand, and the
    egg of the wren,
And the tree toad is a chef d'oeuvre for the highest,
And the running blackberry would adorn the parlors of heaven,
And the narrowest hinge in my hand puts to scorn all machinery,
And the cow crunching with depress'd head surpasses any statue,
And a mouse is miracle enough to stagger sextillions of infidels.
    Walt Whitman

🌷 Welcome to the Moon

Welcome, precious stone of the night,
Delight of the skies, precious stone of the night,
Mother of stars, precious stone of the night,
Excellency of Stars, precious stone of the night.

Anonymous
Translated from the Irish

🌷 The Gardener

His hoe makes a hush
as of a stone rolled away.

We who are standing here
in rows, green men,
small handfuls of death,

we hardly know this one
who tends us—
dark, inscrutable angel
whose step passes by.

John Haines

❦ Coursegoules

Beside the road to Coursegoules
  Are shepherdess and sheep.
The sun is hot. The shade is cool
Beside the road to Coursegoules,
And every man's a fool, a fool
  Who does not fall asleep
Beside the road to Coursegoules
  And shepherdess and sheep.

Frances Cornford

❦ Cock-Crow

Out of the wood of thoughts that grows by night
To be cut down by the sharp axe of light,—
Out of the night, two cocks together crow,
Cleaving the darkness with a silver blow:
And bright before my eyes twin trumpeters stand,
Heralds of splendor, one at either hand,
Each facing each as in a coat of arms:
The milkers lace their boots up at the farms.

Edward Thomas

Lodged

The rain to the wind said,
"You push and I'll pelt."
They so smote the garden bed
That the flowers actually knelt,
And lay lodged—though not dead.
I know how the flowers felt.

Robert Frost

The Brook in February

A snowy path for squirrel and fox,
  It winds between the wintry firs.
Snow-muffled are its iron rocks,
  And o'er its stillness nothing stirs.

But low, bend low a listening ear!
  Beneath the mask of moveless white
A babbling whisper you shall hear
  Of birds and blossoms, leaves and light.

Charles G. D. Roberts

🌷 The Edge of the Island

These stones with myriad surfaces meet the sea,
Polished or faceted by its constant caress,
Standing firm in its shattering spray, to be moved by the plea
Of the tenderly passionate liquid hands that press
Over them searchingly, bringing the pulsing tide.

> *William H. Matchett*

🌷 Magna Est Veritas

Here, in this little Bay,
Full of tumultuous life and great repose,
Where, twice a day,
The purposeless, glad ocean comes and goes,
Under high cliffs, and far from the huge town,
I sit me down.
For want of me the world's course will not fail—
When all its work is done, the lie shall rot;
The truth is great, and shall prevail,
When none cares whether it prevail or not.

> *Coventry Patmore*

🌷 Morning in Madrid

Skirmish of wheels and bells and someone calling:
a donkey's bronchial greeting, groan and whistle,
the weeping factory sirens rising, falling.

Yelping of engines from the railyard drifted:
then, prelude to the gold-of-wine of morning,
the thunderstorm of iron shutters lifted.

Bernard Spencer

🌷 The Pollard Beech

Blue-pencil knife, to keep it brief,
Edits the sprawled loquacious beech,
And clips each hyperbolic leaf
To fit the city's stumpy speech.

Till, like a slogan, trim and terse,
It stands and sums up in a word
The gist of that once epic verse
Whose every branch rhymed with a bird.

Laurie Lee

❧ Aware

Slowly the moon is rising out of the ruddy haze,
Divesting herself of her golden shift, and so
Emerging white and exquisite; and I in amaze
See in the sky before me, a woman I did not know
I loved, but there she goes, and her beauty hurts my heart;
I follow her down the night, begging her not to depart.

D. H. Lawrence

❧ November

Say what you like and say what you will,
   This is an end of decent weather;
The green hide molts from the God-damned hill
   And summer and beauty stalk off together.

Dawn will come late and still too early,
   The imbecile wind will have shutters to pound,
And the best of me will go sullen and surly
   With the bear and the woodchuck into the ground.

Jake Falstaff

❧ To Make a Prairie

To make a prairie it takes a clover and one bee,—
One clover, and a bee,
And revery.
The revery alone will do
If bees are few.

Emily Dickinson

❧ To a Late Poplar

Not yet half-drest
O tardy bride!
And the priest
And the bridegroom and the guests
Have been waiting a full hour.

The meadow choir
Is playing the wedding march
Two fields away,
And squirrels are already leaping in ecstasy
Among leaf-full branches.

Patrick Kavanagh

🌷 Back Yard, July Night

Firefly, airplane, satellite, star—
How I wonder which you are.

William Cole

🌷 Gardeners

So is the child slow stooping beside him
picking radishes from the soil.
He straightens up,
his arms full of the green leaves.
She bends low to each bunch and whispers,
Please come out big and red.
Tugs at them gently to give them time to change,
if they are moody and small.
Her arms filled, she paces
beside her grandfather's elderly puppet walk.

David Ignatow

❦ Tourists

There is nothing to look at any more,
everything has been seen to death.

D. H. Lawrence

❦ Still Lifes—I

Like cool ample breasts
hiding a secret ardor,
the heavy grapes lie near
the brown virile pears.
Consumed by redness
two apples with brazen femininity
nestle close to a glistening
ripe-with-wisdom orange.
A pair of bananas gape like clumsy yokels.
Eagerly,
like a girl after her first kiss,
a cherry breaks away from its red stem.

> Reuben Iceland
> Translated from the Yiddish by Etta Blum

❦ *The Full Heart*

Alone on the shore in the pause of the nighttime
I stand and I hear the long wind blow light;
I view the constellations quietly, quietly burning;
I hear the wave fall in the hush of the night.

Long after I am dead, ended this bitter journey,
Many another whose heart holds no light
Shall your solemn sweetness, hush, awe and comfort,
O my companions, Wind, Water, Stars, and Night.

> *Robert Nichols*

❦ *A Patch of Old Snow*

There's a patch of old snow in a corner
    That I should have guessed
Was a blow-away paper the rain
    Had brought to rest.

It is speckled with grime as if
    Small print overspread it,
The news of a day I've forgotten—
    If I ever read it.

> *Robert Frost*

Spray

It is a wonder foam is so beautiful.
A wave bursts in anger on a rock, broken up
in wild white sibilant spray
and falls back, drawing in its breath with rage,
with frustration how beautiful!

D. H. Lawrence

Prelude

Still south I went and west and south again,
Through Wicklow from the morning till the night,
And far from cities, and the sites of men,
Lived with the sunshine, and the moon's delight.

I knew the stars, the flowers, and the birds,
The gray and wintry sides of many glens,
And did but half remember human words,
In converse with the mountains, moors, and fens.

J. M. Synge

The Early Morning

The moon on the one hand, the dawn on the other:
The moon is my sister, the dawn is my brother.
The moon on my left and the dawn on my right.
My brother, good morning: my sister, good night.

Hilaire Belloc

Absences

Rain patters on a sea that tilts and sighs.
Fast-running floors, collapsing into hollows,
Tower suddenly, spray-haired. Contrariwise,
A wave drops like a wall: another follows,
Wilting and scrambling, tirelessly at play
Where there are no ships and no shallows.

Above the sea, the yet more shoreless day,
Riddled by wind, trails lit-up galleries:
They shift to giant ribbing, sift away.

Such attics cleared of me! Such absences!

Philip Larkin

🌷 Maples in Autumn

The sudden rioting
Of crazed octogenarians
Reeling with ale
Shouting the old damnations
And dancing
Till their coats catch fire.

William Woods

🌷 Stooping for Salad

In the tired yard, with soil
Far too sour for growing much
    Near the high old linden
    Dripping as in sorrow,

My shadow hangs over
The sorrel that I gather
    In the hardening
    Of the afternoon light.

John Hollander

🌷 *Midsummer*

Scarred by the glacier,
Like a tired elephant
An old gray boulder lies asleep
In the woods, in the hollow top
A pool of dark insidious water.

    H. R. Hays

🌷 *A Day in Autumn*

It will not always be like this,
The air windless, a few last
Leaves adding their decoration
To the trees' shoulders, braiding the cuffs
Of the boughs with gold; a bird preening
In the lawn's mirror. Having looked up
From the day's chores, pause a minute,
Let the mind take its photograph
Of the bright scene, something to wear
Against the heart in the long cold.

    R. S. Thomas

🌷 *Fishing Boats in Martigues*

Around the quays, kicked off in twos
The Four Winds dry their wooden shoes
    Roy Campbell

🌷 *Waiting Both*

A star looks down at me,
And says: "Here I and you
Stand, each in our degree:
What do you mean to do.—
      Mean to do?"

I say: "For all I know
Wait, and let Time go by,
Till my change come,"—"Just so."
The star says: "So mean I:—
      So mean I."
    Thomas Hardy

🌷 Nothing Gold Can Stay

Nature's first green is gold,
Her hardest hue to hold.
Her early leaf's a flower;
But only so an hour.
Then leaf subsides to leaf.
So Eden sank to grief,
So dawn goes down to day.
Nothing gold can stay.

Robert Frost

🌷 Exultation Is the Going

Exultation is the going
Of an inland soul to sea,
Past the houses, past the headlands,
Into deep eternity.

Bred as we, among the mountains,
Can the sailor understand
The divine intoxication
Of the first league out from land?

Emily Dickinson

Night

That shining moon—watched by that one faint star;
Sure now am I, beyond the fear of change,
The lovely in life is the familiar,
And only the lovelier for continuing strange.

Walter de la Mare

Discovering God Is Waking One Morning

Discovering God is waking one morning
sun beaming, an east wind blowing,

bees humming on Queen Anne's lace,
lace tilting, bowing in the wind,

and knowing there is more than this.
Now everything is different, better.

The morning sun laughing at shadows
east wind blowing smiles from the sea

Queen Anne bowing greeting in the meadow;
my whole world sings a hymn, awaking.

John L'Heureux

❦ The Way We Live

Having been whipped through Paradise
and seen humanity strolling
like an overfed beast
set loose from its cage,
a man may long for nothing so much
as a house of snow,
a blue stone lamp,
and a skin to cover his head.

> *John Haines*

❦ Good-Night

A latch lifting, an edged cave of light
Opens across the yard. Out of the low door
They stoop into the honeyed corridor,
Then walk straight through the wall of the dark.

A puddle, cobblestones, jambs and doorstep
Are set ready in a block of brightness
Till she strides in again beyond her shadows
And cancels everything behind her.

> *Seamus Heaney*

VIII

*"Don't it
make you
want to cry?"*

those boys ran together
at Tillman's
and the poolroom
everybody see them now
think it's a shame

everybody see them now
remember they was fine boys

we have some fine black boys

don't it make you want to cry?

     -Lucille Clifton

🌷 *The Boss Hires*

I want a man who has nothing to gain.
I want his face to say: nothing more is to be lost.
I want to see from his hands:
That he shall not mind the hours,
That he shall stay on, that the pay will never be just.

     Charles Simic

Sunday Morning

You begin to tell a story.
I perceive it to be
Another of those unpunctuated excursions
Into the country of my failures.
You, pointing to the familiar landmarks.
I, nodding in assent.
We settle back.

Harvey Shapiro

Saeva Senectus

How many nights, in rainy streets, alone
Among the lovers hurrying home to bed,
I fight with enemy time and am not bested,
And stand amid the stricken years like stone.

Lights change and lovers move; and I am left:
Not even remembering who cried, who laughed—
An old man hesitating in the rain,
Lust in the throat and horror at the brain.

T. S. Matthews

❧ The Mother

Of course I love them, they are my children.
That is my daughter and this my son.
And this is my life I give them to please them.
It has never been used. Keep it safe. Pass it on.

Anne Stevenson

❧ Wants

Beyond all this, the wish to be alone:
However the sky grows dark with invitation cards
However we follow the printed directions of sex
However the family is photographed under the flagstaff—
Beyond all this, the wish to be alone.

Beneath it all, desire of oblivion runs:
Despite the artful tensions of the calendar,
The life insurance, the tabled fertility rites,
The costly aversion of the eyes from death—
Beneath it all, desire of oblivion runs.

Philip Larkin

✿ The Great Day

Hurrah for revolution and more cannon-shot!
A beggar upon horseback lashes a beggar on foot.
Hurrah for revolution and cannon once again!
The beggars have changed places, but the lash goes on.

William Butler Yeats

✿ The Smiles of the Bathers

The smiles of the bathers fade as they leave the water,
And the lover feels sadness fall as it ends, as he leaves his love.
The scholar, closing his book as the midnight clocks strike, is hollow
    and old;
The pilot's relief on landing is no release.

These perfect and private things, walling us in, have imperfect and
    public endings—
Water and wind and flight, remembered words and the act of love
Are but interruptions, And the world, like a beast, impatient and
    quick,
Waits only for those that are dead. No death for you. You are
    involved.

Weldon Kees

Love rejected
hurts so much more
than Love rejecting;
they act like they don't love their country
No
what it is
is they found out
their country don't love them.

> *Lucille Clifton*

🌑 *Fantasy*

Tree without a leaf I stand
Bird unfeathered cannot fly
I a beggar weep and cry
Not for coins but for a hand

To beg with. All my leaves are down
Feathers flown and hand wrenched off
Bird and tree are beggar grown
Nothing on account of love.

> *Elizabeth Jennings*

🌢 Accident on the Highway at Night

His mind smears with stars.
Numb, his body is the earth
spilling on itself. Then
eyes: moving mouths: faces flashing
blood. Swaying, the far clear moon.

     William Pitt Root

🌢 The Closing of the Rodeo

The lariat snaps; the cowboy rolls
  His pack, and mounts and rides away.
Back to the land the cowboy goes.

Plumes of smoke from the factory sway
  In the setting sun. The curtain falls,
A train in the darkness pulls away.

Goodbye, says the rain on the iron roofs.
  Goodbye, say the barber poles.
Dark drum the vanishing horses' hooves.

     William Jay Smith

🌷 Aubade

Having bitten on life like a sharp apple
Or, playing it like a fish, been happy,

Having felt with fingers that the sky is blue,
What have we after that to look forward to?

Not the twilight of the gods but a precise dawn
Of sallow and grey bricks, and newsboys crying war.

    Louis MacNeice

🌷 The Watch

I wakened on my hot, hard bed,
Upon the pillow lay my head;
Beneath the pillow I could hear
My little watch was ticking clear.
I thought the throbbing of it went
Like my continual discontent;
I thought it said in every tick:
I am so sick, so sick, so sick;
O Death come quick, come quick, come quick,
Come quick, come quick, come quick, come quick.

    Frances Cornford

❧ *The Passions That We Fought With . . .*

The passions that we fought with and subdued
Never quite die. In some maimed serpent's coil
They lurk, ready to spring and vindicate
That power was once our torture and our lord.

> *Trumbull Stickney*

Yonder see the morning blink:
  The sun is up, and up must I,
To wash and dress and eat and drink
And look at things and talk and think
  And work, and God knows why.

Oh often have I washed and dressed
  And what's to show for all my pain?
Let me lie abed and rest:
Ten thousand times I've done my best
  And all's to do again.

> *A. E. Housman*

I am no Faust: unsalaried my sin;
It is from love I ask the devil in.

   Donald Hall

The Plowman in Darkness

You ask for the Plowman:
He's as much
In the dark as you are,
Stubbing his toes
From age to age
Is working up a
Snorting rage,
Swears he'll beat his plowshare
Into a sword
Come the great and harrowing
Day of the Lord.

   Jay MacPherson

❦ Irish Curse on the Occupying English

May we never taste of death nor quit this vale of tears
Until we see the Englishry go begging down the years,
Packs on their backs to earn a penny pay,
In little leaking boots, as we did in our day.

> *Anonymous*
> *Translated from the Irish by Máire MacEntee*

❦ "Perchè Pensa? Pensando S'inveccia"

To spend uncounted years of pain,
Again, again, and yet again,
In working out in heart and brain
   The problem of our being here;
To gather facts from far and near,
Upon the mind to hold them clear,
And, knowing more may yet appear,
Unto one's latest breath to fear,
The premature result to draw—
Is this the object, end, and law,
   And purpose of our being here?

> *Arthur Hugh Clough*

Small as a Fist

My dead problems
Already have their epitaphs:
Giant agonies—now pygmy dust.

My living problems
Small as a fist
Beat me
Beat me to death.

> *Ryah Tumarkin Goodman*

###

No, the world will not break,
  Time will not stop.
Do not for the dregs mistake
  The first bitter drop.

When first the collar galls
  Tired horses know
Stable's not near. Still falls
  The whip. There's far to go.

> *C. S. Lewis*

Robert

was born obedient
without questions

did a dance called
picking grapes
sticking his butt out
for pennies

married a master
who whipped his mind
until he died

until he died
the color of his life
was nigger

Lucille Clifton

As it will be in the future, it was at the
                    birth of Man.
There are only four things certain since
                    Social Progress began:
That the Dog returns to his Vomit and the
                    Sow returns to her Mire,
And the burnt Fool's bandaged finger goes
                    wabbling back to the Fire.

Rudyard Kipling

🌷 *Portrait*

It was a heartfelt game, when it began—
polish and cook and sew and mend, contrive,
move between sink and stove, keep flower-beds weeded—
all her love needed was that it was needed,
and merely living kept the blood alive.

Now an old habit leads from sink to stove,
mends and keeps clean the house that looks like home,
and waits in hunger dressed to look like love
for the calm return of those who, when they come,
remind her: this was a game, when it began.

Judith Wright

❦   *Good Husbands Make Unhappy Wives—*

Good husbands make unhappy wives
so do bad husbands, just as often;
but the unhappiness of a wife with a good husband
is much more devastating
than the unhappiness of a wife with a bad husband.

> *D. H. Lawrence*

❦   *Unclosing Circle*

The old widow lying alone at midnight,
By habit—still—on her side of the bed,
Can hear across the hall murmuring talk
Of her daughter and son-in-law, also abed;
Not their words, only the sound of things said.

And she remembers how as a small child
Lying awake it was one of her mysteries,
What her father and mother abed were talking about.
Not quite closing a circle of histories,
She falls asleep down a spiral of Christmas trees.

> *Winfield Townley Scott*

IX

"But I call thee blockhead"

❦ *To Flaxman*

I mock thee not, though I by thee am mockèd.
Thou call'st me madman, but I call thee blockhead.

William Blake

❦ *De Trop*

So casually spoken
without a pause for preparation:

but, like the good raconteur
with a small repertoire

he had practised the piquant phrase
which we heard three times in two days;

and that was too much for entente
(though we understood what he meant).

Alan Dixon

Cuttlefish's Books

Those who call Cuttlefish The Coming Man
Say, "*He can write*"—I do not doubt he can;
I dare say, also, he can read and spell,
Do sums not badly, and spin tops quite well.

    Colin Ellis

Vociferated logic kills me quite;
A noisy man is always in the right—
I twirl my thumbs, fall back into my chair,
Fix on the wainscot a distressful stare;
And when I hope his blunders are all out,
Reply discreetly, "To be sure—no doubt!"

    Anonymous
    Nineteenth Century

🌷 Rich Grip-us

Rich Grip-us pretends he's my patron and friend,
    That at all times to serve me he's willing,
But he looks down so sour on the suppliant poor,
    That I'd starve ere I'd ask him one shilling.

    Robert Tannahill

🌷 The Party

So they went, leaving a picnic-litter of talk
And broken litter of jokes, the burst bags of spite:
In comes Contempt the caretaker, eye on ceiling,
Broom in armpit, and with one wide careless cast
Sweeps the stuttering rubbish out of memory,
Opens the shutters, puts out the intimate lamp,
And, a moment, gazes on the mute enormities
Of distant dawn. And far doors bang in mind, idly.

    W. R. Rodgers

Pest

Pipsqueak so scorns his mental betters
In art, in scholarship, in letters,
He tries his best to mortify:
They simply shrug—"Again that fly!"

R. G. Howarth

The Duke of York's Statue

Enduring is the bust of bronze
And thine, O flower of George's sons,
Stands high above all laws and duns.

As honest man as ever cart
Convey'd to Tyburn, took thy part
And raised thee up to where thou art.

Walter Savage Landor

Soft found a way to damn me undefended:
I was forgiven who had not offended.

> *J. V. Cunningham*

 God Sour the Milk of the Knacking Wench

God sour the milk of the knacking wench
with razor and twine she comes
to stanchion our blond and bucking bull,
pluck out his lovely plums.

God shiver the prunes on her bark of chest
who capons the prancing young.
Let maggots befoul her alive in bed,
and dibble thorns in her tongue.

> *Alden Nowlan*

🌷 The Face

A face Sir Joshua might have painted! Yea:
Sir Joshua painted anything for pay . . .
And after all you're painted every day.

Hilaire Belloc

🌷 The Curates

How impeccably well-dressed they are
These curates!
This one's whole body
Is spruced up in a sort of corset
The expression on his face, contorted.

At what cost to himself and to others
Does he spend his whole life suppressing his vital energies.
At what a terrible cost!

John Horder

Gushing Guest

For hospitality Fulsome must thank
Effusively enough to break the bank
Of courtesy: one sentence had been meet.
Does he perhaps require a stamped receipt?

    R. G. Howarth

Were I (who to my cost already am
One of those strange prodigious Creatures, Man)
A Spirit, free to choose for my own share,
What sort of Flesh and Blood I pleas'd to wear,
I'd be a Dog, a Monkey, or a Bear,
Or anything but that vain Animal,
Who is so proud of being Rational.

    John Wilmot, Earl of Rochester

🌷 *Epitaph for a Columnist*

Believing that his hate for queers
   Proclaimed a love for God,
He now (of all queer things, my dears)
   Lies under his first sod.

     Paul Dehn

🌷 *To a Young Poet*

Be heavy, man, as this grave day commands:
Let line by line down, slabs for Moses' hands.
Don't for the Lord's sake crack one lick of wit,
Or, laurels shriveled, you'll be out of it.
On solemn asses fall plush sinecures,
So keep a straight face and sit tight on yours.

     X. J. Kennedy

🌷 *To James Who Would Not Suffer Fools Gladly*

Suffer fools as best you can:
You would be a lonely man,
James, if every fool you knew
Found he could not suffer you.

Colin Ellis

🌷 *Philoctetes*

Magic bow my magic ass—
No one will admit I am a good shot.
Magic bow my magic ass—
They got no magic; they got no class.

Paul Hannigan

❦ *Base Details*

If I were fierce, and bald, and short of breath,
   I'd live with scarlet Majors at the Base,
And speed glum heroes up the line to death.
   You'd see me with my puffy petulant face,
Guzzling and gulping in the best hotel,
   Reading the Role of Honour, "Poor young chap,"
I'd say—"I used to know his father well;
   Yes, we've lost heavily in this last scrap."
And when the war is done and youth stone dead,
I'd toddle safely home and die—in bed.

Siegfried Sassoon

Old Mr. Parvenu gave a great ball,
And of all his smart guests he knew no one at all;
Old Mr. Parvenu went up to bed,
And his guests said good-night to his butler instead.

Corney Grain

On a Farthing-Gatherer

Here lies Jamie Wight, wha was wealthy an' proud,
Few shar'd his regard and far fewer his goud;
He liv'd unesteem'd, and he died unlamented,
The kirk gat his gear and auld Jamie is sainted.

Robert Tannahill

X

🌷

*"All that's
beautiful
drifts away"*

The Old Men Admiring Themselves in the Water

I heard the old, old men say,
"Everything alters,
And one by one we drop away."
They had hands like claws, and their knees
Were twisted like the old thorn-trees
By the waters.
I heard the old, old men say,
"All that's beautiful drifts away
Like the waters."

William Butler Yeats

Upon Shaving Off One's Beard

The scissors cut the long-grown hair;
The razor scrapes the remnant fuzz.
Small-jawed, weak-chinned, big-eyed I stare
At the forgotten boy I was.

John Updike

Girl Help

Mild and slow and young,
She moves about the room,
And stirs the summer dust
With her wide broom.

In the warm, lofted air,
Soft lips together pressed,
Soft wispy hair,
She stops to rest,

And stops to breathe,
Amid the summer hum,
The great white lilac bloom
Scented with days to come.

Janet Lewis

🌷 Grotto, and Recollection

I swam from you through the grotto, it was not cold,
Under its black roof to the far rock, wrote
On the rock treading water your initial with
One finger,
Swam back to you: your small
Stiff nipples
I remember.

Geoffrey Grigson

🌷 Birth Report

When blam! my father's gun began the dash
Of fifty thousand tadpoles for one egg,
I set myself without a leg to leg
Like sixty for the tape. A tungsten flash,
And then my mother in a nest my aunt
Had paid for let me down.
                                    How can so short
A time have worn so dim the birth report
White, Anglo-Saxon, one-half Protestant?

X. J. Kennedy

Newborn

Skin sodden, genitals grotesque, the wail
of a demon, a withered face of fury
above a tiny knotted chest at odds with the world:
how love such a little animal?

but its indignation, its burning sense
of injustice! where is warmth, dark,
pulses of sustenance? why have they gone?
It is pity that possesses one at first.

And then, peaceful for the moment at the breast,
see the promise of beauty, the downy skull
—a furnace to the cheek—the arctic blue
of eyeballs. It will become human yet.

Molly Holden

🌷 The Bonnie Broukit Bairn

Mars is braw in crammasy,
Venus in a green silk goun,
The auld mune shak's her gowden feathers,
Their starry talk's a wheen o' blethers,
Nane for thee a thocktie sparin',
Earth, thou bonnie broukit bairn!
—But greet, an' in your tears ye'll droun
The haill clanjamfrie!

Hugh MacDiarmid

braw: handsome, splendid
crammasy: crimson
wheen o' blethers: pack of nonsense
broukit bairn: pale-faced child
greet: weep
clanjamfrie: collection, shebang

On the Life of Man

What is our life? A play of passion,
Our mirth the music of division.
Our mother's wombs the tiring-houses be,
Where we are dressed for this short comedy.
Heaven the judicious sharp spectator is,
That sits and marks still who doth act amiss.
Our graves that hide us from the searching sun
Are like drawn curtains when the play is done.
Thus march we, playing, to our latest rest,
Only we die in earnest, that's no jest.

Sir Walter Raleigh

Tiring-houses: stage dressing-rooms

❦ *One Times One Is Eight*

Either old magic or new math
Into our house has beat a path.
How else could Einstein or Diogenes
Explain an exploit of our progeny's?
While at the table with his ilk
A child upsets a glass of milk.
The glass held half a pint when filled,
And half a gallon when it spilled.

Ogden Nash

❦ *For Jane Bradley with a Porringer*

Never may your games be drawn,
Always may you lose or win,
May you not be a looker-on
But a partaker-in;

Not dwell in life's remote suburbs
But in her centers and her towns
And speak her great affirming verbs,
Not just her abstract nouns.

Hal Summers

❦ Cradle Song

Sleep, my baby, my own!
Canst hear the little wheel turn?
Canst hear thy mother abaking and making
The butter come bright in the churn?
And sweeping and singing alone?

Sleep, my little, my dear!
The children are gone to the fair.
The farmers are gone to the clearing, and shearing
The wee little sheep with white hair.
So sleep, my little, my dear.

Janet Lewis

🌷 When Maidens Are Young

When maidens are young, and in their spring,
Of pleasure, of pleasure, let 'em take their full swing,
   Full swing, full swing,
And love, and dance, and play, and sing,
For Silvia, believe it, when youth is done,
There's naught but hum-drum, hum-drum, hum-drum,
There's naught but hum-drum, hum-drum, hum-drum.

    Aphra Behn

🌷 I Remember

It was on my bridal night I remember,
An old man of seventy-three
I lay with my young bride in my arms,
A girl with t.b.
It was wartime, and overhead
The Germans were making a particularly heavy raid on Hampstead.
Harry, do they ever collide?
I do not think it has ever happened,
Oh my bride, my bride.

    Stevie Smith

❦ The Two Parents

I love my little son, and yet when he was ill
I could not confine myself to his bedside.
I was impatient of his squalid little needs,
His labored breathing and the fretful way he cried
And longed for my wide range of interests again,
Whereas his mother sank without another care
To that dread level of nothing but life itself
And stayed day and night, till he was better, there.

Women may pretend, yet they always dismiss
Everything but mere being just like this.

Hugh MacDiarmid

And the days are not full enough
And the nights are not full enough
And life slips by like a field mouse
        Not shaking the grass.

    Ezra Pound

 from *Biography for Traman*

        Let us record
The evenings when we were innocents of twenty—
How, scientists and poets alike, we then
Had the world bottled for our own: not quiet,
Disturbed and bitter, surely, but in hand.
How the girls' breasts were small and firm beside us
When in the evening we walked the campus streets
Under the elm-dark air, sweetened with spring.
How the girls cried with love under the bushes
And we lay scared with our lust, delirious.

    Winfield Townley Scott

✿ North

Already it is midsummer
In the Sweden of our lives.

The peasants have joined hands,
They are circling the haystacks.

We watch from the veranda.
We sit, mufflered,

Humming the tune in snatches
Under our breath.

We tremble sometimes,
Not with emotion.

Donald Justice

🌸 Ages of Man

As foolish as monkeys till twenty or more;
As bold as lions till forty and four;
As cunning as foxes till three score and ten;
Then they become asses or something—not men.

Traditional rhyme

🌸 The First War

Soldiers wore puttees, then. That was
why so many died, were heroic—even
why they had the war. Their legs marching
(I was that high, a speculator about how
tall the world was) had that mysterious
spiral look. General Pershing had such
tight puttees that his wing pants didn't wrinkle
and his ouch face used a little mustache
to hide pain. After the war they had the Armistice,
unwound their puttees, and had legs again.

William Stafford

XI

"When I consider life"

🌷 Life

When I consider life, 'tis all a cheat;
Yet, fooled with hope, men favour the deceit;
Trust on, and think tomorrow will repay:
Tomorrow's falser than the former day;
Lies worse; and while it says, we shall be blessed
With some new joys, cut off what we possessed.
Strange cozenage! None would live past years again,
Yet all hope pleasure in what yet remain;
And from the dregs of life think to receive
What the first sprightly running could not give.

    John Dryden

🌷 Early Astir

Early, early I walked in the city:
The river ran its strength from misty valleys
And the sun lit the wings of stone angels.

Yarrol! Yarrol! I cried exultingly:
Passing dogs lifted wet noses
And housemaidens the blinds of their gables.

    Herbert Read

🌷 Envoi from The Contemplative Quarry

God, thou great symmetry
Who put a biting lust in me
From whence my sorrows spring,
For all the frittered days
That I have spent in shapeless ways
Give me one perfect thing.

Anna Wickham

🌷 The Proof

Shall I love God for causing me to be?
I was mere utterance; shall these words love me?

Yet when I caused his work to jar and stammer,
And one free subject loosened all his grammar,

I love him that he did not in a rage
Once and forever rule me off the page,

But, thinking I might come to please him yet,
Crossed out *delete* and wrote his patient *stet.*

Richard Wilbur

By all means use sometimes to be alone,
Salute thyself: see what thy soul doth wear.
Dare to look in thy chest; for 'tis thine own:
And tumble up and down what thou find'st there.
Who cannot rest till he good fellows finde,
He breaks up house, turns out of doores his minde.

>*George Herbert*

 Athens, Ohio, 1939

"ATHENIA TORPEDOED," says today's
Press in the tourist guesthouse. "WAR IMPENDS."
Out back in the black meadow, among friends—
Some summer bugs contending, timothy's
Familiar dip and scratch behind bare knees,
The duty pool of stars—I can't believe
In such disaster being broadcast, such
Mere alien, unpermitted anarchy
Loosed on an ordered world that features me.

>*L. E. Sissman*

❦ One Sunday
A Grandfather's Tale

One Sunday, when the quick rain fell,
what happened by a scarcely dampened dusty road
on grass still dry under an oak
is that they heard the restless bay mare
snort and stamp, jangling her harness
while their buggy stood in silence, halfway home,
and I was born in earshot of the next spring's Sunday bells.

   William Pitt Root

❦ Short Moral

When Elder Foxx, wed thirty years that night,
stood late behind his window looking at
the icicles that seemed like fragile bars
and saw (across the square) the one who typed
his letters slip and fall—did he pick her up,
Dear Lord, and soothe her cool bruised knees and touch
his cheek to hers, climbing Mrs. Snyder's wicked stairs?
No, thank God, he turned around and found
the camphor sheets of Mrs. Foxx's proper bed.

   Gary Gildner

Man and wife the night resume
In the safety of their room.

On a shelf six stories high,
Like a pair of shoes they lie.

Several hours after dawn
Life will come and put them on.

Edward Newman Horn

 Bronxus

people around here all
the time walking their
dogs even at seven in
the morning Leave it
alone don/t walk your dog
so much
      it/ll
fall off my sainted
mother might have said.

Joel Oppenheimer

An Answer of Sorts
(to Louis Simpson)

Born to the suburbs,
Born to this wasteful middleclass life,
A neighbor sings in her small backyard.

As if she were in a procession
To the temple. She has simply forgotten herself
In the roses. Let her be. Let her be.

Leonard Nathan

North Beach Alba

waking half-drunk in a strange pad
making it out to the cool gray
  san francisco dawn—
white gulls over white houses,
  fog down the bay,
tamalpais a fresh green hill in the new sun,
driving across the bridge in a beat old car
  to work.

Gary Snyder

🌼 Bravado

Have I not walked without an upward look
Of caution under stars that very well
Might not have missed me when they shot and fell?
It was a risk I had to take—and took.

    Robert Frost

I fear to take a step; along the edge
    Of this precipice on which we balance, bearing our burdens,
    Fingers appear, clutching; they are the climbers
    From below, as we were, to this ample ledge.

    May be when we go higher, on to some plateau
    Filled with flowers, we will stop and reach
    Down to their hands as once one stooped to ours.
    But now I fear to step, to see the faces
    Of those who take the fingers under their heels.

Josephine Miles

from *As in Their Time*

Citizen of an ever-expanding
Universe, burning smokeless fuel,
He had lived among plastic gear so long
When they decided to fingerprint him
He had no fingerprints at all.

    Louis MacNeice

What inn is this
Where for the night
Peculiar traveller comes?
Who is the landlord?
Where the maids?
Behold, what curious rooms!
No ruddy fires on the hearth,
No brimming tankards flow.
Necromancer, landlord,
Who are those below?

    Emily Dickinson

Oh, the beautiful child! and oh, the most happy mother!
   She in her infant blessed, and in its mother the babe—
What sweet longing within me this picture might not occasion,
Were I not, Joseph, like you, calmly condemned to stand by!

     Johann Wolfgang von Goethe
     Translated from the German by Arthur Hugh Clough

🌷 *Old Florist*

That hump of a man bunching chrysanthemums
Or pinching-back asters, or planting azaleas,
Tamping and stamping dirt into pots,—
How he could flick and pick
Rotten leaves or yellowy petals,
Or scoop out a weed close to flourishing roots,
Or make the dust buzz with a light spray,
Or drown a bug in one spit of tobacco juice,
Or fan life into wilted sweet-peas with his hat,
Or stand all night watering roses, his feet blue in rubber boots.

     Theodore Roethke

🌷 *To My Daughter*

Not counting the little kids
you shock everyone you know
calling me Gary and Judy Judy
no one thinks it's natural
let alone healthy so we
better keep the pleasure
we get from filling your balloons
with water and squirting the dogs
when they come to lick us
in the tub, quiet, lover.

Gary Gildner

🌱 from *Stella's Birthday*

This Day, whate'er the Fates decree,
Shall still be kept with Joy by me:
This Day then, let us not be told,
That you are sick, and I grown old,
Nor think on our approaching Ills,
And talk of Spectacles and Pills;
Tomorrow will be Time enough
To hear such mortifying stuff.

Jonathan Swift

🌱 *Street Scene: St. John's Wood*

A boy with a motor bike
Races his engine.
Showing off

For a slim tall girl
In blue scrubbed jeans
Whose legs as she stands

Spell shapes
From alphabets
Not taught in schools.

Gerard Benson

🌳 Farm Child

Look at this village boy, his head is stuffed
With all the nests he knows, his pockets with flowers,
Snail shells and bits of glass, the fruit of hours
Spent in the fields by thorn and thistle tuft.
Look at his eyes, see the harebell hiding there;
Mark how the sun has freckled his smooth face
Like a finch's egg under that bush of hair
That dares the wind, and in the mixen now
Notice his poise; from such unconscious grace
Earth breeds and beckons to the stubborn plough.

      R. S. Thomas

🌷 *Things Men Have Made—*

Things men have made with wakened hands, and put soft life into
are awake through years with transferred touch, and go on glowing
for long years.
And for this reason, some old things are lovely
warm still with the life of forgotten men who made them.

> *D. H. Lawrence*

🌷 *Heaven—Haven*
(A Nun Takes the Veil)

I have desired to go
Where springs not fail,
To fields where flies no sharp and sided hail
And a few lilies blow.

And I have asked to be
Where no storms come,
Where the green swell is in the havens dumb,
And out of the swing of the sea.

> *Gerard Manley Hopkins*

🌷 Thel's Motto

Does the Eagle know what is in the pit,
Or wilt thou go ask the Mole?
Can Wisdom be put in a silver rod?
Or Love in a golden bowl?

William Blake

🌷 Days

What are days for?
Days are where we live.
They come, they wake us
Time and time over.
They are to be happy in:
Where can we live but days?

Ah, solving that question
Brings the priest and the doctor
In their long coats
Running over the fields.

Philip Larkin

❦ Timeo

Dear God (safe ambiguity)
If I address you faithlessly
The fear of heaven devils me.
Could I be sure of purgatory
Sure I could praise and not adore thee
I might a tepid faith embrace.
But I am terrified of grace.
Gethsemane is any place.

Isabella Gardner

❦ Virtue

In these old hackneyed melodies
Hollow in the piano's cage
I see the whole trash of the age—
    Art, gadgets, bombs and lies.

Such tunes can move me to confess
The trash moves, too: that what offends
Or kills can in its simplest ends,
    Being human, also bless.

Roy Fuller

The show is not the show,
But they that go.
Menagerie to me
My neighbor be.
Fair play—
Both went to see.

Emily Dickinson

Without Laying Claim

without laying claim
to an impossible innocence
I must tell you how
in the midst of that crowd
we calmly pulled the pins
from six grenades
mumbling an explanation
even we didn't believe
& released the spoons
a lump in our throats

William Wantling

I said to my heart between sleeping and waking
Thou wild thing that always art leaping or aching.

Lord Peterborough

❦ *Upon the Downs*

Upon the downs when shall I breathe at ease,
Have nothing else to do but what I please?
In a fresh cooling shade upon the brink
Of Arden's spring have time to read and think.
And stretch, and sleep, when all my care shall be
For health, and pleasure my philosophy?
When shall I rest from business, noise, and strife,
Lay down the soldier's and the courtier's life,
And in a little melancholy seat
Begin at last to live and to forget
The nonsense and the farce of what the fools call great?

Attributed to Edmund Ashton

❦ The Wall Test

When they say "To the wall!"
and the squad does a right turn,

where do you stand? With the squad
or the man against the wall?

In every case
you find yourself standing against the wall.

Louis Simpson

❦ To the Accuser Who Is the God of This World

Truly, my Satan, thou art but a Dunce,
And does not know the Garment from the Man.
Every Harlot was a Virgin once,
Nor canst thou ever change Kate into Nan.

Tho' thou art Worship'd by the Names Divine
Of Jesus and Jehovah, thou art still
The Son of Morn in weary Night's decline,
The lost Traveller's Dream under the Hill.

William Blake

🌷 Christmas Eve Wish

This year, Santa, I want
To glide like a swallow.
I want to fit myself
Like an ice cube in its tray,
And do something when added to water.

> David Steinglass

🌷 Housewife

Some women marry houses.
It's another kind of skin; it has a heart,
a mouth, a liver and bowel movements.
The walls are permanent and pink.
See how she sits on her knees all day,
faithfully washing herself down.
Men enter by force, draw back like Jonah
into their fleshy mothers.
A woman *is* her mother.
That's the main thing.

> Anne Sexton

Below the surface-stream, shallow and light,
Of what we *say* we feel—below the stream,
As light, of what we *think* we feel, there flows
With noiseless current strong, obscure, and deep,
The central stream of what we feel indeed.

    Matthew Arnold

🌷 *Passing Remark*

In scenery I like flat country.
In life I don't like much to happen.

In personalities I like mild colorless people.
And in colors I prefer gray and brown.

My wife, a vivid girl from the mountains,
says, "Then why did you choose me?"

Mildly I lower my brown eyes—
there are so many things admirable people do not understand.

    William Stafford

❦ Gold Watch at Sixty

Retired so early; what's living for?
A flashlight burning in a drawer.

William Cole

❦ On King William III

As I walk'd by my self
And Talk'd to my self,
My self said unto me,
Look to thy self,
Take care of thy self,
For nobody cares for Thee.

I answer'd my self,
And said to my self,
In the self-same Repartee,
Look to thy self
Or not look to thy self,
The self-same thing will be.

Anonymous
Seventeenth Century

INDICES

Index of Poets

Index of Titles

Index of First Lines